The Spirit and Power of Elijah

The Spirit and Power of Elijah

PROPHETIC PARALLELS OF THE
ANCIENT PROPHETS AND LEADERS OF TODAY

DON LYNCH

© Copyright 2005—Don Lynch

All rights reserved. This book is protected by the copyright laws of the United States of America. This book may not be copied or reprinted for commercial gain or profit. The use of short quotations or occasional page copying for personal or group study is permitted and encouraged. Permission will be granted upon request. Unless otherwise identified, Scripture quotations are the author's own translation of the Bible. Please note that Destiny Image's publishing style capitalizes certain pronouns in Scripture that refer to the Father, Son, and Holy Spirit, and may differ from some publishers' styles. Take note that the name satan and related names are not capitalized. We choose not to acknowledge him, even to the point of violating grammatical rules.

DESTINY IMAGE® PUBLISHERS, INC.
P.O. Box 310, Shippensburg, PA 17257-0310

"Speaking to the Purposes of God for this Generation and for the Generations to Come."

This book and all other Destiny Image, Revival Press, Mercy Place, Fresh Bread, Destiny Image Fiction, and Treasure House books are available at Christian bookstores and distributors worldwide.

For a U.S. bookstore nearest you, call 1-800-722-6774.
For more information on foreign distributors, call 717-532-3040.
Or reach us on the Internet: www.destinyimage.com.

ISBN 10: 0-7684-2590-5

ISBN 13: 978-0-7684-2590-1

Previously published as *The Spirit and Power of Elijah* by Ministry Matrix, Jacksonville Florida

For Worldwide Distribution, Printed in the U.S.A.

1 2 3 4 5 6 7 8 9 10 11 / 09 08 07

Acknowledgment

To Ruthanne, my dear wife, best friend, and partner in ministry; and our awesome three sons, John Michael and his wife, Mandy, James David, and Jared Paul.

Endorsement

I was challenged by the prophetic message of *The Spirit and Power of Elijah* and encouraged by Don's testimony of transformation in revival. Thousands of leaders like Don and Ruthanne are being raised up in these last days. Brenda and I both read this book and believe it accurately locates where the Church is.

You will be challenged as well. Anticipate what is coming next. Get ready for what God is doing in your generation! Don't miss your place in the next move of God.

Reverend John Kilpatrick
Pastor, The Church of His Presence
Daphne, Alabama
Conference Speaker and Author
Pastor of Brownsville Assembly
during the Brownsville Revival

Contents

	Introduction............................ 11
1	Why Elijah?........................... 25
2	The Seasons of God................... 41
3	Unlikely People and Places 65
4	Today's Prophetic Leaders 77
5	Prepare the Lord a People 91
6	Presence-Driven Leaders 115
7	Elijah Prayer and Worship........... 127
8	Our Time of Visitation 147
Conclusion	Revival and Restoration.............. 161
Appendix	The Vision of Jesus Claiming His Church 169
	Ministry Information 183
	Ministry Resources.................. 187

Introduction

During the centennial celebration of the Azusa Street Revival, Ruthanne and I were in Los Angeles with some of this generation's pioneering leaders sharing the strategies Jesus is giving His Church for the next season. God spoke to me specifically about visiting Azusa Street while we were there, that He had a personal revelation for us about revolutionary revival. Exciting stuff!

We found the site of the Azusa Street Mission but only after careful searching (real men don't ask for directions). It is now a red brick alley with only a small sign that has been hit by a bus, nearly obscured by growing trees. More than 700 million people worldwide look back to this location because the outpouring that began there exploded into the earth, a fire that burns even more brightly now than it did then.

As we stood there on the site, Ruthanne began to weep and I was deeply moved by Jesus' promise that what happened there would happen again in a greater way; that He would not leave out this generation, and that we would see, hear, and experience another mighty wave of Holy Spirit's power!

More than a century ago, Jesus visited His Church in an obscure mission on Azusa Street in Los Angeles, California. It was an unlikely place where unlikely people were touched in unlikely ways to fulfill unlikely purposes. That revolutionary revival opened a wellspring that fed a restoration river for decades. For 100 years, hundreds of millions walked into that stream, part of the greatest harvest to date.

Many of our best missiologists and greatest leaders were convinced this was the last, end-time harvest; it is natural to experience this kind of unprecedented spiritual visitation and see it in ultimate terms. However, I believe this restoration river and harvest created the army Jesus is now preparing for revolutionary revival and harvest of even greater magnitude and dimension!

What we thought was the great harvest produced an army of harvesters Jesus is now empowering to lead a greater worldwide expansion and establishment of His Kingdom.

Whenever Father is changing seasons and Jesus is coming for a visit, He sends forerunning leaders to prepare His people. Prophetic leaders accurately anticipate what is coming next and prepare God's people before it arrives. Prophetic people are more in tune with "what is coming next" than "what is."

When I write about the spirit and power of Elijah, I am not referring to prophecy gift operations, nor am I speaking only of prophets in a simpler, localized sense. I am talking about something new.

I am describing prophetic leaders sent by God to the Body of Christ to prepare a prophetic people for the "next level" and the "next wave." I am describing these prophetic leaders as the prophetic element of the fivefold ministry, a foundational leadership function of the Body. Whether or not their message is received by the majority at first, these leaders must be recognizable as prophetic leaders.

As this prophetic leadership is introduced, a remnant feels uncomfortable with "what is" and begins reaching for "what is coming next." This generation is experiencing the discomfort and discernment of a prophetic people. Their dissatisfaction with "church as usual" reveals both the need for radical change in the way we "do church" and the heart of Jesus for revolutionary revival.

The new prophetic leadership is here! America is filled with millions of saints ready for "what is next" who feel disenfranchised, discontented, and dissatisfied with "what is." Some of them misunderstand their spiritual quest, their unwelcome passion, their painful rejection. All prophetic leaders and people come out of a wilderness as the time of visitation approaches.

Each of us must look forward to the coming revolutionary revival with an eye for what revolution looks like. We must live as prophetic people ready for Jesus' next strategic visitation. We must receive this disruption of confrontational leadership or we will find ourselves fighting with Jesus.

One hundred years ago, Jesus used unlikely people in unlikely places to prepare His people for a century-long restoration. He is doing it again!

It is hard to picture the Church without Azusa Street's revolutionary revival; and looking forward, we should not only expect another visitation and welcome anything and everything Jesus sends us, we should also expect and embrace radical changes before it comes.

This is the spirit and power of Elijah prophetic leadership.

REVOLUTIONARY REVIVAL

Revolutionary revival is coming to the Church! Millions of people will experience the presence of His glory, and Jesus will lead His Church beyond the deadening and stifling organizational limitations of conventional "churchanity."

Revolutionary revival will begin outside conventional church through awakened revolutionaries. A new prophetic leadership will emerge both outside and inside conventional church. Remnants will be created both inside and outside the conventional church. Existing conventional church leaders will be transformed within conventional church; emerging revolutionary revival leaders will be transformed outside conventional church. When the two meet, the unusual spiritual authority and power of transformational leadership will explode!

We put labels on outpourings of God's presence in order to more conveniently discuss why and how they began. In a few decades, we will be looking back at this generation's revolutionary revival and discussing why and how God visited certain places and people.

Prophetic leaders are everywhere preparing prophetic people for God's visitation. Their leadership will get us ready for what God is doing next.

I am identifying prophetic leadership as "spiritual leaders who accurately anticipate what Jesus is doing next and prepare people before it arrives." The outbreak of prophetic leadership will not be limited to well-known, visible leaders; it includes a regiment of hidden leaders walking out of their wilderness preparation to lead remnants of revolutionary Christians.

God wants you to experience prophetic leadership in your own life. Since the beginning of all leadership is personal leadership, prophetic leadership beings in personal prophetic leadership.

Jesus Picks Up the Church

It was a vision of vast proportion, unlimited spiritual perspective. In it I could see Jesus among "the churches" in the same way John saw Him walking among the seven churches of Asia in the Revelation. Different from John's vision, however, I could see Him walking among the churches in the nations of the earth. I knew Jesus was among His people. The revelation was nearly overwhelming—millions of believers in thousands of cities.

Something in the vision alerted me that Jesus was dealing with the whole Body of Christ. The perspective was universal. I was seeing the church everywhere at the same time. I could see Jesus walking among them, standing tall, powerful, and ready for action. He was huge! In every sense, Jesus was present, interacting with the Body, more than enough as our Head, Intercessor, and King.

Then, I saw this mighty Jesus reach down and pick up the global church. It was not a building as I would naturally visualize "church." (The Body of Christ is not a building of any architectural type or model.) I saw Jesus reach down and pick up the whole church.

When He did, everything inside began shaking, moving around, and changing. Nothing could stay "in place" while the Church was in the Master's hand. He knelt down with the Church in His left hand while extending His right hand out to lay new foundations. Then He set the Church back down on these new foundations.

I was amazed at the reaction of the people and leaders inside. Some started immediately looking around to locate the old stuff, trying to put it all back where they wanted it. A few looked out the windows hoping to get some idea of what had happened. Still fewer seemed aware of the implications of Jesus' actions.

Many did not believe that Jesus was the One who had caused the shaking, or that new foundations were laid in place by His hands. They had an attitude that "God wouldn't do that" regarding changes to the status quo.

Then I heard voices lift above the commotion. People paused to listen and everything became quiet. The voices were explaining in strong, confident tones that Jesus had picked up the Church and put new foundations under it. They explained that the old furnishings and decorations were not to be put back in place, that Jesus had both a new look and sound for His Church.

Many dropped what was in their hands and left the old stuff where it was—chairs lying on their sides, tables turned upside down, and broken pictures lying at the baseboard where they had fallen off the walls. But some faces turned angry and some voices were heard demanding everything be returned to its "proper places," declaring that anything less would be a violation of "a holy place."

Mostly people just ignored these demands and stood waiting for the new stuff to arrive. When the angry voices became louder, they moved away from them and waited in corners or against the walls while these angry folks struggled with all the piles of discarded paraphernalia.

It was a season of waiting. A time when many of God's people could see the old wasn't working anymore. They were anticipating the new.

Today's Prophetic Leaders

Prophetic leadership engages and enforces God's decisions. Emerging at the leading edges of expansion, these leaders operate in the spirit and power of Elijah to prepare a people for what the Lord is doing here and now.

Prophetic leaders lead the shaken Church in establishing new strategies for a new season. Their voices are heard amid the confusing clamor of transition telling us Jesus is the One shaking His Church and restoring its foundations. They reveal and release God's decisions, and have authority and responsibility to see them properly and fully executed. They help build upon the new foundations, reset by Jesus, so the Church can push past the old and into the new.

Prophetic leadership is foundational leadership. It is leadership that helps order the Kingdom for its greatest influence and impact. Prophetic leadership prepares a waiting people for the next move of God. The preparation process broadens exponentially during the transitional generation once it is introduced.

Many Christians feel guilty about their lack of passion for conventional church. They feel condemned that they are waiting and preparing for the next season. This condemnation is not from God. Without prophetic leadership, leadership attempts to wrestle people into ministry changes by intimidation and manipulation based on defective definitions of "church," "ministry," and "discipleship," the very things Jesus is redefining by resetting the foundations of His Church.

A Leadership Movement

The spirit and power of Elijah rests upon and creates a leadership movement. This movement is already evident and continues to mature as a global influence within the Church.

Prophetic leadership is inherently confrontational and transformational. It seems to confront everything—bad and good—but it transforms all. Prophetic leadership challenges "what is" with "what is coming next" so we will be ready to respond to Jesus' leadership in the next season. Prophetic leadership is all about Jesus being more involved in leading His Church than ever before! Prophetic leadership is all about what Jesus is up to next.

Transformation is key. Change is coming whether or not we are ready! We must get ready for the biggest changes of our lives. It is no longer a question of whether revolution is coming…it is already here! It is now a question of whether or not we will be ready to lead in that altered condition.

Whether or not we will run into tomorrow's revolutionary revival with passion for the purpose of Jesus or grind in our heels against any change in status quo will depend upon our preparation for the next season. It will be a question of responding to the leadership of Jesus in a season of shaking and sifting.

Some of the most important international leaders in the Church have documented the inevitability of changes already at work, changes that will create revolution in this generation. This revolutionary revival is the work of Jesus. It is a question now of being ready to respond to Him or clinging stubbornly to our comfortable traditions.

The momentum of the Body of Christ should always be toward what is coming next. "What is" has been given resources to feed momentum for "what is coming next." Old wineskin organizations should be empty when the time comes for new wineskins and new wine.

Wineskins are not people, they are organizations filled with and led by people, but not the people themselves. Wineskins receive resources to build and feed momentum, but they should be empty when the new wine arrives.

I am calling this next move of God "revolutionary revival" because it is not the renovation of the old wineskin. Old wineskins usually lack interest in being emptied out. They struggle to maintain something for their purposes that Jesus designs to be invested in His purposes. Immediately when revival occurs, old wineskins want to own its momentum in order to perpetuate the very things Jesus sent revival to change.

Jesus is picking up His Church, removing the old foundations, and setting it down on new ones. Foundational leaders are identified as "apostles and prophets" in the New Testament; and whenever foundational leadership is reset, something greater than revival is released because the revival becomes a revolution.

This revolutionary revival represents Jesus claiming His Church. Jesus is saying, "I love you, but this is My Church and I will do with it whatever I want."

Prophetic leadership allows Jesus to be more involved in leading His Church than any other leadership paradigm. Apostles and prophets are foundational. The restoration of the apostolic and prophetic foundations to the Church Body will provide the foundations for the most effective prophetic leadership the Church Body has ever known!

Jesus is coming in this season to claim His Church and lead it into the next season. This is a "day of the Lord" moment. This is a new season for new wine. This is a day of visitation in the truest sense of the New Testament. This book will also help you understand what is happening here and now in the Church and set you in place to be a prophetic person, prepared to do what God has created, called, and gifted you to do in the coming season of revolutionary revival.

Jesus As a Warrior

In March 2003 I experienced a life-changing prophetic vision during a ministry training class. I have included a fuller version later in the book, but I want to share a portion here because it illustrates how Jesus is changing His Church in this season.

[Carried up in the spirit and hovering over nations of the earth, I could see Jesus standing up to claim His Church.]

"I see the Lord rousing Himself as a Mighty Warrior, rousing Himself in power and authority. He is awesome, as the Scriptures say, "terrible," in the sense that He creates terror and awe in those who witness His presence and glory.

"He is shaking Himself, shaking off what settled around and upon Him. He had allowed these conditions to continue in mercy, to settle like dust upon the earth and remain in place. I see Jesus shaking Himself, shaking off these natural conditions. They have rested upon Him, as sifted dust settles upon an immobile object."

[Jesus was standing. In the vision, Jesus had been lying there, covered with centuries-old dust, waiting.]

"He is shaking Himself, arousing Himself. The Psalmist says, 'Stand up, Oh God!' Jesus is standing! The dust of centuries is shaking loose from Him, and a mighty wind blows it away as if it had never been.

"It is not that Jesus has been inactive. This is what Scripture describes as kairos times, as 'days of the Lord.' We are approaching another 'day of the Lord' in history when God is revealed and His purposes are reestablished. Jesus is revealing Himself among the nations, and the hearts of many will be shaken. Men will be weak with terror at what He is doing."

[Jesus stood completely upright now. He set His feet and looked around challenging everything and everyone. His eyes were flames of fire and He was dressed as a warrior. He was claiming the land for His Kingdom purposes! As He challenged all other claims, mighty angels began standing with Him!]

"As the Lord is rising, mighty angels rise all around Him, rising with Him. He is Lord of hosts, Lord of armies. Rising with Him are resting angels, not really dormant as much as simply hidden, waiting.

"This is happening in every nation of the earth, but especially in the Americas—Central and South America extending into North America."

When Jesus Comes to His House

My first grade attempt at phonics and printing my name were built upon my kindergarten mastery of tying my shoe laces and included a marvelous little poem by Joan Gale Thomas. In those days, no one would complain when Mrs. Alexander mentioned the name "Jesus" in school, and she read this poem to us more than once.

I can still remember the opening phrases:

"If Jesus came to my house and knocked upon the door; I'm sure I'd be happier than I've ever been before."

The general mood is cute and homey, like sketching Jesus sitting down to tea and crumpets in a child's playroom. Great stuff for children! Jesus visits them in gentle, everyday ways.

Now, in my more mature years, walking in prophetic awareness, the picture of divine visitation is very different, especially after experiencing Jesus standing up in the nations to claim His Church.

"If Jesus came to His house and knocked upon the door; I'm sure I'd be more *shaken* than I've ever been before."

Scenes of Him entering the temple and basically turning everything upside down come to mind! The first places He would go are the very ones we wish He would ignore. The first things He would change are the ones we are most proud to display as representative of our ideas, wisdom, and creativity.

Church is Changing

"Church" is changing. The next season will be one of startling and uncomfortable change. We must change to be changed. We need to be the Church instead of a giant apparatus maintaining something that should have been emptied out by now. Without prophetic leadership, we protect status quo and remain unprepared to follow Jesus as He moves into a new season.

Some of the Church's most respected leaders and authorities on the state of the Church have analyzed the present American Church and given us a baseline to measure its future successes. They conclude that going forward doing the things we are doing now will result in further spiritual and natural decline. Investing technology, marketing, manpower, and resources in "more of the same" will not improve performance.

Revolutionary strategies and tactics that embrace radical changes are absolutely essential. What we did to get where we are now will not get us to where Jesus is going next. Jesus is doing something new and we must get ready to do church differently to fulfill His strategy in the new season.

This is why God sends prophetic leaders to get His people ready for the next season. He wants them prepared for what is coming next. He wants His people with Him as He moves on to establish the Father's will. Jesus does not want to leave anyone behind!

1

Why Elijah?

Here and Now

What can we learn from the fact that God has made Elijah's spirit and power available today to His people? Why Elijah? What of his life, character, and actions has God preserved and reserved to prepare revolutionary leaders for revival?

For several years since experiencing revolutionary revival in my own life, Jesus has been teaching me about the kind of leadership He wants for His Church and the radical changes He will make in the Body to get what He wants in this generation. There is a reason God started something with Elijah that He wanted to remain available for His people.

The spirit and power of Elijah is a leadership anointing. Elijah's leadership was confrontational, transformational, and prophetic. Elijah authority and power is available here and now to prepare a people ready for God's visitation today, as it was available and operating in John the Baptist preparing a people ready for Jesus.

God is releasing this kind of prophetic leadership as He introduces a new level of authority and power. A season of visitation is coming that will release revolutionary revival. This harvest will originate in nations prioritized by revolutionary revival, cultures prepared by prophetic leadership to respond to what God is up to in this generation.

The spirit and power of Elijah prepares a prophetic people ready to respond to what is about to happen.

The seasons are Father's business, but getting ready for Father's next season is the business of prophetic leaders. The Church is not prophetic unless focused upon what God is up to here and now. When the Church is expending massive energies and monies to get what it wants, unaware or unconcerned with what God wants, it becomes painfully obvious that God's people lack prophetic leadership. The Church is not prophetic when it fails to prepare people and leaders for the coming season before that next season arrives.

Right now, God's house is full of leaders straining at their stocks, out-of-step with preprogrammed purposes, revolutionary leaders whose demanding destinies and pressing passion demand something beyond what is, because they are already experiencing what is coming next.

Sometimes I think I will explode if I hear one more conference presentation on church growth models, attendance gimmicks, small group programs, marketing dynamics…

Here it is—everywhere, all over the United States, people are feeling like "there must be something more" and they are searching for it—"no matter what it costs and where I have to go to get it."

Why Elijah?

There is an ever-increasing movement away from "church as usual." The trend toward the next season has begun and gained far too much momentum to be stopped. Whether we like it or not, the change is here and more is coming!

Elisha Picks Up More Than a Mantle

Two prophetic giants walked out of the shadows cast by the hot desert sun, taking the final steps of a journey that would finish the leadership of one while launching the leadership of the other. They were oblivious to the suddenly swirling winds and the sting of blown sand. They had been moving toward this moment for days.

The older one, Elijah, was hairy and rugged, alone when in a crowd and dauntingly intimidating in his demeanor. His face was engraved with the danger and drama of determined encounters with hell's highest heathens. The other, Elisha, was noticeably younger, reddened and weathered by too much sun, his face exposed to the elements by receding hair, his eyes quick to pick up movement on the bland, barren horizons.

The swirling winds increased, air pressure spiked, and static electricity clicked between grains of desert sand. The fiery chariot of Israel's angelic army appeared and separated them. The seasoned prophet, Elijah, would be carried away in the whirlwind, hair blown wild in its tumbling crosscurrents, any last final words torn from his lips and lost in the roaring swirl.

But the younger Elisha was there! After days of extending his stay with the aging prophet, passionate for destiny, he now knew God had included him in Elijah's translation. He knew something of double measure was coming to him and looked up expectantly…

In the grip of a terrible blast, the older prophet loosened his hold on his mantle, the decorated and sacred instrument of his intimacy with Jehovah, a simple yet powerful garment, bedroll, and covering. For a brief moment, it was stretched out like an empty canvas.

Then the twisting winds tore it away like an unwieldy kite weighed down with a tail of enormous destiny, and it appeared that it might be blown away forever. The whirlwind suddenly spit it out like a mouthful of offending fish bones, and the mantle of Elijah floated down to earth and landed at Elisha's feet.

The mantle did not fall upon him. He reached for it—and claimed more than a familiar piece of fabric, a remnant of his relationship with a mighty man of God. Elisha picked up an available anointing! He returned equipped to fulfill a work of prophetic leadership that he had shared with the elder statesman of Heaven. Now he must carry that work into a new season of fullness and fulfillment. A firstborn's double portion now rested upon him, for he had received a double portion of spirit.

Elisha slapped the mantle on Jordan's waters, and said, "Where is Elijah's God?" The waters piled up to one side and left a dry path just as they had for Elijah. The mantle then took on a broadened significance, beyond Elijah and the double portion, beyond even Elisha's ministry being unpacked for fulfillment with that initial miracle. (See 2 Kings 2.)

The mantle has been unfurled again and again throughout history, whipped by winds of reformation, a banner of revolutionary revival. From that moment, the spirit and power of Elijah has remained available for the prophetic leadership.

Malachi's last words to Israel, sustaining God's people for 400 years of prophetic silence, echoed against cold walls of despair: "Listen, God's people, Elijah is coming—sent by God before the dawning of the Lord's Day." (See Malachi 4:5.) Malachi announced, "The spirit and power of Elijah remains available these many, many years after Elisha's death. This mantle of prophetic leadership will visit us again!"

The power of prophetic words and the spirit of prophetic ministry remained in the earth to prepare people for days of heavenly visitation.

In Jesus' day, John the Baptist was the voice, the prophetic leader, the way-preparer operating in the spirit and power of Elijah; but the mantle of Elijah, the spirit and power of Elijah, was not buried with John's headless body. Jesus picked it up and carried its message and ministry to heights to which we can only stagger with our lips turning blue in the thin atmosphere of spiritual revelation.

The spirit and power of Elijah is available today!

The Ancient Cathedral

In this vision, I am walking along the outside walls of a very large cathedral constructed of native stone by building methods three or four centuries past. I enter through a side door usually available only to professional clergy. I enter near the front, in the vicinity of the altar.

Here I see religious rudiments representative of several sacred Christian systems.

No one particular flavor of Christian institutionalism dominates, for it seems to represent them all. While many traditional trappings of religious order are obvious and operational, everything in the vision is black and white except two specific things I can see in full color—water baptism and the Lord's Table.

Jesus is with me. I hear Him say, "These are the only 'anointable' things in this place." This simple, singular statement opens my spirit to an understanding, an unveiling revelation of God's heart.

Experiencing the vision, my heart asks, "The only anointable things? Everything else is not anointable?" The revelation is rather shocking to me because I have lived all my life believing what happens "in church" is done for Jesus, in His Name, and by His will. I have believed it is all anointable because it is all done for Him.

In the vision, the religious trappings of the cathedral all appear black and white. They are nonexistent in God's mind, only distractions from what is real. It becomes apparent that water baptism and the Lord's Table are not the only things Jesus wants to anoint, but they are merely the only things in that cathedral that are "anointable."

Jesus says, "Not everything of tradition is worthless, just most of it! While the Church has wandered far from My design and desire, I have preserved the essence of that design and desire. I will restore its true meaning in your generation. Look for the anointable things. Don't be distracted by human source and resource. It's not anointable."

Anointable Things

Jesus is restoring the anointable things, restoring the essence of "church." It is not that He will destroy what man has substituted as much as He will simply ignore it. Because it is so irrelevant, He will act as if it doesn't exist. In the cathedral, I noticed water baptism and the Lord's Table were tokens to men because these were not anointed when men used them in religious rituals.

Busy, busy, busy—Jesus ignores our billion-dollar busy-ness—it is the mark of a religious spirit, the substitution of human source and resource for the Cross and Holy Spirit. Our substitution brings to mind the scariest verse in the Bible where Jesus says, "Many will say in the day, 'Lord, Lord haven't we done wonderful stuff in your Name, and then, I will say, 'Who are these people and how'd they get in here? Get them out of here!'" (See Matthew 7:22.)

What is incidental to man may be of supreme importance to Jesus. Some anointable things continue as form without power in conventional church, the little that remains in its total operation and organization that Jesus would anoint; many things in conventional church are simply worthless, dead works.

The cathedral in my vision represented the church in history. It was about 400 years old, about the same amount of time that passed between the last prophet, Malachi, and the days of John the Baptist. When John came preaching to prepare a people for Jesus, his prophetic leadership was nothing short of revolutionary, occurring outside the established institutions, confrontational and transformational to the core.

Jesus started where John left off and carried prophetic leadership to its fulfilling heights. He then passed it on to His Church. The momentum of Jesus' leadership carried the Gospel into the ends of the earth in the days of Paul, John, and Timothy.

That spiritual momentum has been reset, restarted, and released. We are the generation that will have opportunity to walk in great spiritual momentum. We are not leaving anything behind but carrying into the next season all that the Father has restored in the last 400 years. We will have the opportunity to bring that spiritual momentum to fullness.

Fullness

The fullness of the Church in the fullness of the Spirit in the fullness of time. Some of our best leaders are bringing us a perspective of this reality. After decades of statistical study and analysis of church in the United States, the terms "radical and pervasive change" are being defined. Research uncovers undeniable trends in America away from faith practices based on the dead rituals of that ancient cathedral, the subtly advanced substitution of human source and resource for the authority and power of God.[1]

Millions of believers, born again and sold out to real Christian living, are walking away from every flavor of church that builds on old wineskin systems, programs, and organizations. They are practicing their faith in bold, fresh ways that represent a radical, revolutionary shift in the way believers "do church." Their revolutionary behavior will bring revolutionary revival and create the most pervasive and expansive change in the Church we have seen for 400 years.

Something awesome and huge is shifting in the spirit that will restart the ministry and anointing Jesus invested in His Church at Pentecost. A foundational leadership shift is underway that will create momentum in the Body of Christ for what is coming next. This restart will also shift people, resources, money, energy, and focus toward revolutionary revival. It is too late to discuss whether the shift is a good idea, a God idea, or a plot hatched in hell. The shift has been happening for years and gaining momentum.

I believe Jesus is the One who started the trend, and He is the One feeding its momentum toward radical change.

The Spirit and Power of Elijah

Since the days of Elijah, God has been sending His people leaders who can prepare them for His visitation. Visitation is one of Father's seasons, a time when Jesus gets extremely "upfront and personal" with His people.

When the spirit and power of Elijah is at work, we know Father is getting us ready for a visit. Jesus described His ministry as a season of visitation: "Your house is left unto you desolate because you did not recognize the time of your visitation." (See Luke 19:44.)

Visitation is an inspection, and an accounting is required by the owner of those who have been in charge of his enterprises. We derive the title "bishop" from this word, an "overseer" responsible for God's property. The sense of the term is that the owner seems absent in some seasons while those He has made responsible take care of his property. Then a season of visitation comes; the owner shows up to see how well those in charge have done.

Revolutionary revival happens when Jesus, the Bishop of the Church, arrives to personally make a claim upon what is His. We are living in a season of preparation for such a visitation. This visitation season will continue in segments of the Church for the next several years.

Jesus is walking among the churches again! Now, the spirit and power of Elijah is operating in prophetic leaders He is sending ahead of Him to prepare a people ready to respond when He arrives. The spirit and power of Elijah confronts all that God isn't going be happy with when He shows up. It brings many changes. Some of the changes will be painful.

Hold onto your hat! Some of the biggest changes in church history are coming in this generation! Your eyes will see it. Your ears will hear it. You will experience it. Get ready!

God is sending prophetic leaders so you can be ready. Every city will feel the shaking of this preparation season. It will not come to every place at the same time, so the season of preparation will continue spreading across the earth for many years. During this time, prophetic leaders will dominate the landscape of church leadership.

Everyone will be asked to change. Everything will move more closely to God's design and purpose. Things are out of order. To get them back into order, we must change and be changed. The spirit and power of Elijah operates in spiritual power to effect such spiritual transformation.

The spirit and power of Elijah is here and now operating in the United States, calling her to revival and restoration. Millions of American believers know this is a time for something spiritually powerful. They also understand God needs to change the Church because "church" has not and cannot provide America what she needs. Many Americans know that only Jesus can bring this nation what it needs, and millions of church-attending believers are looking outside conventional church for God.

Prophetic leaders initiate change. Although we usually wait two or three generations after they are dead to applaud them, they are heroes in Heaven while they do the will of God here and now.

Why did God choose Elijah to start this revolutionary revival preparation movement? Why is the spirit and power of Elijah the prophetic mantle Father sends to prepare a people ready for divine visitation? In the following chapters, I will explain how the Elijah mantle works today and how we can walk in the restoration that the spirit and power of Elijah brings.

Of all God's previously chosen leaders whose mantles have disappeared, the spirit and power of Elijah is available today. Why not Samuel or Daniel or Isaiah? Why did God send John the Baptist in the spirit and power of Elijah? And, why is this anointing still available within the Church, resting upon those whom Jesus calls to prepare people for His visitation? Why is Jesus releasing the spirit and power of Elijah here and now, lifting up transformational leaders who challenge deeply-seated traditions and religious conditions?

God singled out Elijah, marked his character and anointing for future leaders of future generations, and gave Elijah something He wanted available in other seasons and other nations. God saw something vital in the spirit and power of Elijah that we should passionately desire in our generation.

I remember a vivid prophetic experience that I received about the restoration of God's reserved and preserved purposes, a vision that included Elijah and vastly increased my understanding of why Jesus has restored worship, intercession, and prophetic leadership to us in this generation.

Twelve Men of Restoration Vision

[After he was crowned King over Israel and Judah, David parked the Ark of the Covenant on a high hill above Jerusalem. The ark had been left a few miles away after the initial disastrous effort to bring it to Mount Zion on an oxen-drawn cart.

In the vision, Jesus came up beside me and nudged me with His elbow.]

"Let's visit David's tent of meeting," Jesus said.

I could see the tent in front of me. As we moved to the opened side of the tent, I could see that the tent was filled with glory.

Entering David's tabernacle, I was immediately overwhelmed with sight, sound, and smell. I could smell glory. I could taste glory. I could hear glory. I experienced glory.

Why Elijah?

Worship was as fragrant as incense! I could smell the sound. The sound of worship was a living, breathing atmosphere of His glorious presence. I saw that when music, dance, and incense are blended in spiritual worship—the sound smelled, the dance sang, and the incense fragrance vibrated with sound!

The ark dominated the canvas courtyard. I stood looking at it, aware of the glory of God all over the structure. The ark was there, but the glory was everywhere!

Jesus said, "I am rebuilding David's tent. I am bringing back what my people lost by substituting their worship for mine. What David established for me was only a physical shadow of true spiritual worship. This true spiritual worship will be real in my people again."

Jesus indicated the ark with a gesture: "You can see that I am bigger than a box." He laughed as if sharing "a funny" with a friend.

[Then, I could see something changing in my perspective, like a camera swinging into a different position in a movie scene. I was consciously aware of the ground between me and the ark.]

I saw two rows, 12 men lying down as if buried, six on either side with their feet toward the center aisle. In the vision, everyone seemed aware that these 12 men were part of the whole set up.

As I looked on, each of the 12 men stood up one after another in order of their appearance in history. Each had been a leader and represented a different period of history. Samuel was one. Elijah was another. And, some were men from more recent history, four or five hundred years ago. All were leaders in different seasons of God's visitation.

Each had been a kingdom leader whose influence had been etched into previous spiritual generations. Some had swords and shields, dressed in medieval-type clothing. Samuel still had his mantle draped around his shoulders. Elijah did not.

Jesus said, "Each of these men represents a season of visitation. None of what they released into my people has been lost. They all await a generation that will fulfill what they started, will bring to fullness what they released in their generations. I have preserved and reserved what they released for fulfillment in this generation. I am restoring all these mantles of leadership in your lifetime. The generation that sees the restoration of David's tabernacle will also see the fullness of the Church."

Two rows of six men now stood in straight lines facing one another. I looked straight on between the two rows. As I looked on, Elijah stepped out from the row of men on the left and raised his two hands in the air as if to start something, as if to call an orchestra to attention, start a choir singing an anthem, or shout "gentlemen, start your engines!" at a race.

Jesus said, "These are days of restoration of all. There are many Elijah's, Samuel's, and Wesley's now. Not one or two, here and there—many. I have multiplied prophetic influence to touch every people everywhere in this generation."

ELIJAH SETS THE NEW IN MOTION

In the vision, Elijah raised his hands to start something, orchestrate something, begin a song or start a race.

Why Elijah?

The gesture represented all these things to my mind and explained more fully the function of the spirit and power of Elijah. Elijah gets things going! His preparation leads to the next step, the next season, the beginning of a fundamental shift in spiritual conditions.

During his life and ministry, Elijah represented a season of visitation in which Jehovah held out the possibility of complete restoration to His people. Elijah represented the call of God to His people in the midst of terrible rebellion, spiritual blindness, idolatry, and Jezebel's treachery. It was a call to restoration. It said, "No matter how bad things are, Jehovah sees the possibility of total restoration of the purpose of God in this culture."

Prophetic leadership represents the leadership God gives His people in the season in which they are living. It represents and reveals what God is doing here and now.

Endnote

1. George Barna, among others, has accumulated 25 years researching trends that reveal Americans moving away from religious systems and institutions into revolutionary spiritual behaviors. For greater detail, see Barna's books, *Revolution* and *The Frog in the Kettle*, and *Changing Church* by C. Peter Wagner.

2

The Seasons of God

How Prophetic Leadership Works

Prophetic leadership is about what is coming next more than what is. If your leadership is about preparing people for what already is, you are not leading prophetically. You are maintaining something Jesus is already turning into something else.

Prophetic leadership whispers intimately to individuals, declares to a generation, and fog-horns to entire cultures. All prophetic leadership operates according to the Father's season. So, prophetic leaders are unique.

Prophetic leadership that can prepare it to fulfill something that has been accumulating for centuries has been given to each generation. When previous generations fail to fulfill the purposes of the seasons assigned them, Father preserves and reserves them for a future, faithful generation. Father's purposes will all be fulfilled! None will be lost!

Father's preserving and reserving has an accumulative effect, and prophetic leadership prepares us to move the whole pile of spiritual history forward. Prophecy is always about fullness and fulfillment: fullness is the fulfillment of purposes left unfulfilled by previous generations in our culture. Ultimately, Jesus fulfills all Father's purposes, but each prophetic leader's ministry reveals a unique strategy for the Father's season in the culture and generation to which they have been assigned.

Jesus has created each of the world's cultures to provide something unique to the Kingdom of God. That unique, divine purpose is the reason for that culture's very existence. Prophetic leaders help to restore that purpose. Prophetic leadership finishes something Jesus started. Prophetic leaders are all about reaching in and pulling out what Jesus has put in.

THE SEASONS OF GOD

Prophetic leaders give us signals and clues to what God is up to in our generation. They lead consistent with the Father's strategy for the season. Prophetic preparation is a demanding process because Jesus is getting us ready for fullness and fulfillment. While it is always difficult for us to change, to get ready for season changes, we must get ready or face the possibility of failure!

Seasons are in the Father's hands. Jesus recognizes the Father's seasons and the required strategy that will fulfill the season's purpose. "Seasons of God" reflect the ways Father deals with a culture at a given time; seasons reveal how God has chosen to deal with us.

One of the most significant revelations of Scripture is the revelation of how God deals with man. God reveals Himself and His ways in the Bible so we will recognize Him when He involves Himself in history. When God does something, we should be able to say, "Look, I know who that is! That's God. That's how God does stuff."

Jesus explains seasons as part of Father's strategy to manifest the Kingdom: Father has "Kingdom establishing" strategy in mind for every season in every culture and generation.

Just before Jesus ascended into Heaven, Jesus met with His disciples. They asked Him when the Kingdom would be restored to Israel. He explained that this was the wrong question. (See Acts 1:6-8.)

Jesus answered them against the backdrop of Israel's cultural and redemptive purpose: to establish God's Kingdom in the earth, to be witnesses of His glory and Kingdom to the whole earth. Then He clarified the Church's required response to the next season of the Father.

Jesus says, "You won't know all times or seasons the Father sets by His own authority, but you will receive power when Holy Spirit comes upon you. Then, you will be My witnesses in Jerusalem, all Judea and Samaria, and to the whole earth."

Or in other words, "Father will do whatever He has determined with Israel in this season, but you will be given the responsibility to establish the Kingdom of God in the earth by a different means and strategy as My witnesses. You will be given spiritual authority and power."

It became apparent that whatever Father has determined to do with Israel, the Church remnant was being prepared to fulfill the purpose of God, a purpose preserved and reserved for fulfillment, a purpose Jesus came to empower personally for fulfillment through His Body, the Church.

We can know Father has times and seasons for our generation and culture. We know Jesus will prepare us to participate with Him in fulfilling the strategic purposes of the Father's season, the season in which we live. We must be prepared before the season arrives, prepared as prophetic people by prophetic leaders to prophetically anticipate what is coming next.

Jesus did not say we would never know what Father is up to, so we should just go on blindly doing what we have always done (as good excuse as any to avoid change and just do what we want).

No! Jesus says, "Receive power and then go as my representatives. You will be ready to work with the Father to fulfill the strategic purposes of Father's season in each culture you visit: Jerusalem first, then ever-expanding expeditions into every culture on earth." (See Acts 1:8.)

Father's Season for Your Generation

Jesus is getting us ready for season change. He is sending prophetic leaders in the spirit and power of Elijah. He is getting us ready to respond to the next season before that season arrives. That's how prophetic leadership works.

Often God's people resist prophetic leadership because they really don't want season change, and they don't want to personally change to fit Father's next season. They want Father to change His mind! This has been the identifiable stubbornness of God's people for generations. This spirit often leaves only a remnant ready for the purposes of the Father.

Embracing the transformation needed to be ready for the next season releases tremendous favor into our lives. We are then empowered and equipped in measure equal to the season we are assigned to lead.

Jesus uses the phrase "this generation" more than 20 times in the Gospels to identify the one in which He lived and based His ministry and leadership exclusively upon the Father's season for His generation. He taught His disciples to walk in the authority of Father's season and the power of Holy Spirit to fulfill His strategic purposes wherever they went. Jesus ministered in the Father's season. He ministered in a grace flow of favor and perfectly invested that grace flow in what His Father wanted.

This is the prophetic sense of life and living, the prophetic sense of ministry and leadership. As you lead and minister in your generation, your leadership must fulfill the strategy for the Father's season. To do this, you must be prophetic! You must discern prophetically what Father is up to here and now.

When conventional church leaders copy others, mark trends, measure success in terms of existing ministry models, and use "what is" to determine what Father is doing in their generation, they lead people away from what Father is doing instead of releasing them into it. Prophetic leaders see what is coming next and prepare people before it arrives. Many leaders identify Father's seasons by what is and miss what He is about to do because they fail to lead prophetically. For this reason they and the people they lead may not be ready for the next season.

Right now, millions of prophetic people are walking away from this kind of leadership, seeking something that will awaken, prepare, release, and order their lives for what is coming next. Like David's army, they are mighty men and women of the next season hidden in wilderness preparation. They are all about what is coming next for the Church. They are the disenfranchised and discouraged, worn out, driven out, and spit out of conventional churches because they don't fit what is. They are mighty men and women of what is coming next.

Understanding seasons help us see our generation and culture from Father's point of view. Leadership must always be freshened with the coming season's revelation. Leaders lead because they know where to go. Prophetic leaders know where to go because God reveals the next season to them. They know to prepare those following them to live and minister in the next season before that season arrives.

You must be able to discern the season of your generation so your leadership prepares people to respond to Him. And, you must have prophetic leaders in your life, people who accurately anticipate the Father's season for your generation and culture.

More than program tweaks, personality traits, principle treatments, and purpose trends—you must be a prophetic leader here and now. This is not leadership as usual, and the prophetic Church will not look like "church as usual."

The Seasons of God

Prophetic Leaders are Assigned Unique Ministries

My good friend, Manoel Alberto, lives in Sao Paulo, Brazil with his wife and two daughters. Because he is my good friend, I am compelled to speak wisdom into his life. He is one man living with three women—that requires wisdom.

I say, "Manoel, I am going to share some wisdom that may both change and save your life. Three things you need to know about women. You live in a home with three women. You need this wisdom."

I hold up three fingers. "Three things every man needs to know about women." He stares at my three fingers, drunk with hope. I want to shake him and say, Pay attention, man, you are hanging from a thread here!

"Number one. You ready?" One finger punches the air. His hand unconsciously lifts as if to grasp hold of that one finger, then settles back to his lap.

"Manoel, women know what they want." He receives it! Nodding sagely, a thousand mundane experiences suddenly come together in his psyche, a brilliant chorus singing the same note, a ballad of a man, a husband, a father, a hu-man-be-ing! A woman's will imprints upon her world. Red-hot steel hammered by the shocks of resolve. He knows this song.

"Women know what they want." Two fingers rise before his face. His tongue wets his dry lips as the aura of epiphany fills the room—fragrant osmosis, light bulbs bursting in a four-block radius, insects suddenly silent in the dark, city night [proverbially speaking, of course].

"Second, women will tell you what they want." He sees it now! Women do know what they want, and they tell you what they want. In a myriad varieties of coded messages as subtle as the angle of the head, the constriction of the pupils, the faintest inflection of a vowel. The horse whisperer is a babe in the woods by comparison.

"They will tell you what they want, my friend." Manoel slaps his face, hand wiping down to his mouth to catch the drool. I reach with one finger to close his jaw, save some dignity; briefly he recovers, but gravity wins again. Revelation can be so unnerving.

"Number three!" The cadence of my voice rushes and seems to fill the room with thunderous sound. Night birds fall silent. Lights dim. Was that time itself pausing to sigh? Three fingers. Final words.

"Women get what they want!" Meteors shower. Angels sing. Galaxies shrug. Thomas Edison appears above Manoel's head to turn on the first light bulb ever made. A local manufacturer starts his presses. A messenger's service enters the room to present him with the first women-get-what-they-want T-shirt.

It is obvious now that he knows. He whispers, "Yes, I see it! My wife. My babies. My family. My life. Now, I can truly be a man!"

A bit of humor there. (Could you tell?) To illustrate something eternal, I exaggerated a bit since the weight of revelation is too great for words to bear. To understand prophetic leadership, we must begin with God. He knows what He wants. Then, He speaks what He wants to those who can make it happen. By Divine commandment, whatever it takes, one way or the other, God gets what He wants.

Prophets of Bible history were not all the same. We categorize them based upon what they did, said, wrote, and the time and conditions in which they were prophetically active. Each was unique. Our categorizations explain and identify them more than something intrinsic to their ministries.

All prophets were called to get God something He wanted specific to the season they were assigned. Some were especially obedient; others only partially or painfully fulfilled limited aspects of their calls. Prophetic leadership varied because prophetic leaders were ministering to fulfill the various strategies of the Father's seasons. Prophetic leaders were unique to the season in which they served and lived.

In the case of Moses, God wanted a slave generation released and resettled upon their heritage. Along the way, He wanted to reset the foundations of their culture, restore the purposes of their nation, and reestablish their assignment to be a light to every nation on earth. Through Moses, His prophetic leader who entered the process from the outside, Jehovah brought a new political order to a people enslaved by taskmasters, transforming them into a nation of warrior priests, and preparing them to live in their homeland once they arrived.

Moses does all this prophetically. Without models or existing examples, by revelation and prophetic leadership, Moses fully prepares a people for the Lord, a people led by new leaders, novel cultural mores, a unique spiritual assembly, with a backdrop of prophetic experiences that give their new culture a storyboard for future generations.

In David's day, God wanted to make a kingdom people of Israel. Along the way, He wanted to reset the entire cultural and spiritual foundations upon kingship in anticipation of Messiah. Through David, His prophetic leader who entered the process from the outside, Jehovah rallied and equipped a people without weapons, transforming them into worshipping warriors, and preparing them to be the greatest expression of Messianic kingdom in history.

David did all this prophetically. He ignored models and existing examples of heathen cultures around him and fully prepared a people for the Lord, reset the foundations of the spiritual and cultural assembly, established the priesthood, the worship, the Tent of Glory, and left them a framework of shared prophetic experiences, music, and stories that continue to prophecy of Messiah's kingdom to this day.

All prophetic leaders are assigned a season. Their assignment is to get God something He wants in that season. They must get God what He wants in that season by leading people. More than anything else, prophetic leaders get God the people He wants.

Define "purpose" as "what God wants." Define "prophetic" as "God tells us what He wants." Then, define "leadership" as "get God what He wants." Hebrews 1:1 says that God has always known what He wanted throughout history, speaking to us in many various ways at different times through prophets serving Him. In these last seasons, God introduced Jesus, His Son, to speak in a new, fresh way, and reestablished what He wants, redefined prophetic leadership.

God is giving you the prophetic leadership you need to develop prophetic leadership within yourself and be prepared to respond to God's visit in your generation.

Father wants to get something into your life and leadership. Father wants to get something from your life and leadership. Father wants to get something through your life and leadership. He provides you a leadership foundation upon which to build the fulfillment of purpose. Without that foundation, you will surely miss the purpose of Father's season.

You may do a million wonderful things in His Name; but if you don't get God what He wants in your generation, you will have merely played religious games.

Father favors what He wants. He invests favor in His purposes. He invests favor in the leaders He assigns to prepare for the next season. He invests favor in preparation for the next season before that season arrives.

The Bible says, "Noah found favor in the eyes of the Lord." God sent animals from all over the earth to Noah's boat. Try doing that without favor!

Prophetic Leaders for This Season

Some prophets spoke into special and specific conditions, both narrow in focus and brief in duration. Others were prophets of events more relevant to future history than their own generations, responsible to paint panoramic landscapes with bold, broad brushstrokes. Still others were prophetic leaders who altered history by their inspiration, influence, and impact.

Prophetic leaders were not all the same in biblical times. They are not all the same now. To stereotype prophetic people, prophets, and prophetic leaders is to categorize them by human standards, creating expectations foreign to their special callings.

Today, Jesus is sending prophetic leaders of the Elijah caliber who have authority and responsibility to establish, execute, and fulfill God's decisions. He is releasing them within various regions with authority and responsibility to help transform people, churches, cities, and entire cultures. He is teaming them with other foundational leaders and restoring the ministry of Jesus.

The spirit and power of Elijah is available for every leader. God has assigned leaders to be ready and get others ready for a season of visitation. Leaders need to pray prophetically, rear children prophetically, serve the Body prophetically, and live, breathe, and think prophetically because this is a season of preparation.

The next season will be one of Kingdom building and harvest. Jesus is visiting His Church, and His visitation will bring change and course correction to the whole Body. A season change is moving across the earth as we experience harvest. To get us ready, a new kind of leader is needed, and a new kind of leadership is rising.

This "next-step leadership" is foundational and transformational. I believe that prophetic leaders with unusual authority and power to engage and enforce God's decisions are arriving. Their leadership is emerging at the leading edge of Church growth around the world. They are foundational, helping reset the Church's foundations; they are transformational, helping restore transformation to the Church's ministry.

Prophetic leaders reveal and release God's decisions and have authority and responsibility to see them properly and fully executed.

Declaring and Enforcing God's Decisions

Prophetic leaders declare God's decisions, what the Scriptures call His "judgments." They communicate God's opinions, which the Scriptures call "His ways, testimonies, statutes, laws, and ordinances." When these judgments and opinions have been established as the shared and common beliefs and values that motivate the behavior of a people, that people begins to live as a Kingdom culture.[1]

God sent prophetic leaders to His Kingdom culture in Israel. They fulfilled a special kind of ministry that uniquely represented God in the earth.

Elijah was one of these special leaders. His ministry enforced God's decisions and called Israel back to its cultural purpose. Elijah's ministry occurred during a season of restoration. He declared that God's decision was to restore Israel's calling and purpose in his generation, not destroy it. He provided foundations for revival, although Ahab and Jezebel, Israel's king and queen, refused to build cultural transformation upon those foundations.

In his Elijah ministry, John the Baptist laid foundations for a new season of restoration in Israel, but the leaders of Jesus' generation refused change, refused transformation, refused the Father's season. Jesus said, "They have done with John whatever they wanted." He also said, "Your house is left to you desolate because you did not know the time of your visitation." The leaders of Jesus' generation missed Father's season!

Right now, Father is preparing His people for a season change. He is sending prophetic leaders who have unusual transformational authority and power. This is the prophetic leadership He is giving us in this generation because restoration is God's heart for us!

Many contemporary leaders compare this revolutionary revival with the Reformation that startled Europe in Martin Luther's generation, the civil rights revolution in the United States, and the impact of feminism in terms of its scope and impact upon culture. The tide is rising in America. Revolutionary revival will impact every institution in our culture and completely alter how our beliefs govern our lifestyles.

EXECUTING GOD'S JUDGMENTS

The Hebrew word *mishpat*, translated "judgment" means "to receive an order and execute that order." It assumes authority to rule and to administer God's decisions. Judgments refer to kingdom decisions; and when the king makes a decision, his people carry out his wishes, following their appointed leader. This is the sense of kingdom leadership.

The Church's mission is to establish God's Kingdom on earth. It is one thing for church leaders to hand down edicts, bark out orders as CEO's of church corporations—it is another for their leadership functions within the Church to execute and carry out *God's* decisions and opinions. Many leaders identify their titles as marks of their assignments, basing their authority upon human definitions, but "leader is as leader does." If leaders aren't getting Father what He wants, they aren't establishing His Kingdom.

God has His own system for identifying and measuring success—He measures how well leaders are carrying out the decisions of the King. His leaders must know what He wants and know His heart in wanting it. This kind of leadership requires the authority and power of the King for success; no human authority or power qualifies anyone for position or title, nor can it create success.

Mere leadership is not enough. The devil's a leader! Title and appointed position are not enough. Ahab had position. Jezebel was a leader! Leaders are everywhere; but leaders who know and enforce God's decisions and opinions must be prophetic leaders. It is God's leadership we are looking for, leadership that gets Him what He wants. That is Kingdom leadership!

Prophetic leaders do more than announce God's decisions; they have authority and power to see that they are carried out. They help carry out and execute God's judgments motivated by God's opinions. They work with other leaders but must do more than make announcements and pronouncements about God's decisions and opinions.

Elijah didn't make empty claims; God's Kingdom decisions in Elijah's day were not only expressed with words but also in power. Elijah prayed and it didn't rain! That's power and authority. Elijah didn't "ask nice" if King Ahab would consider God's point of view. His prophetic leadership brought Israel to the mountain of confrontation and released transforming fire.

Prophecy is all about fulfillment, about doing what is prophesied. While there are prophets who are not leaders but solely serve to announce God's decisions and opinions, God is sending prophetic leaders to this generation who have authority and power to execute God's strategies.

Prophecy and judgment is what Jesus was telling us to declare about when He taught us to pray, "Heavenly Father we worship Your Name. Kingdom of Heaven, arrive! Will of God, happen!" (See Matthew 6:9-13.) God's decision is His judgment, and the execution of that judgment is foundational to the Kingdom rule of God.

Notice the wording of the phrase that describes David: "And David reigned over all Israel; and David executed judgment and justice unto all his people." (See 1 Chronicles 18:14.) David executed judgment. He carried out decisions that released justice to his people. This was the picture of Messiah's kingly rule that John the Baptist came to prepare Israel to receive.

The mishpat, or judgment decision, of God's perfect ruling authority could only be executed in the earth through the authority and power of Jesus. It must be executed now through the Church, and Jesus is restoring the foundations of Kingdom authority and power in this generation!

Prophetic Leaders Have Authority and Power

Jesus had the Kingdom keys but gave them to men. Jesus could bind and loose—limit and expand, destroy and restore, withhold and release—in Heaven and earth, but He gave His leaders that authority and responsibility to do on earth what had already been done in Heaven.

This is Kingdom-of-Heaven authority, the authority Jesus gave His first leaders. He gave the keys of the Kingdom to mankind, and *kingdom* means rule, govern, order, and execute.

Jesus prophesies to Peter: "Let me tell you who you really are, Peter. You are a little chunk of rock. But upon this massive, substrata rock foundation—Me, God's Messianic King—I will construct My called-out assembly, My Church. The authorities of hell will not be able to withstand its construction, and I will give Heaven's Kingdom keys to you. You will prohibit in the earth whatever has been prohibited in Heaven and release in the earth whatever has been released in Heaven." (See Matthew 16:18-19.)

Jesus runs the mission and ministry of His Church through leaders. His leaders have authority and power to know what He wants and do what He wants. Jesus manages His Kingdom through Kingdom leaders.

The Kingdom is not the same thing as the Church. Jesus gave the Kingdom keys to His leaders because the Church has a mission to establish Kingdom culture in the earth. Church leaders must first be Kingdom leaders. We have lost many Kingdom aspects of the Church's mission and ministry, but Jesus is coming to reestablish His Lordship in the Church. We are experiencing a revival of the Lordship of Jesus!

This clarifies the mandate of prophetic leadership. In the greater Kingdom conflict between light and darkness, the Church has Kingdom authority because the Church is on God's side! The Kingdom is the greater structure that the Church is to establish and manifest.

There is a Kingdom clash over who controls these cultures. The Church positively presses for the Father's purposes and runs into and over the opposition of hell's authority and rulers.

Prophetic leaders fulfill a leadership role in declaring and enforcing God's decisions. We will struggle in descriptions and definitions during this time of restoration. It is a healthy struggle. We are working to redefine leadership during a leadership paradigm shift in which leaders who declare and decree prophetically have accompanying leadership responsibility to enforce and execute God's revealed decisions and opinions.

These new leaders have responsibility to coordinate spiritual restoration and societal transformation. Prophets declare and decree, but prophetic leaders must do more—they must help enforce and execute. They have to. They are foundational, transformational leaders. Leadership definitions are being restored, and we must change our behavior to fit the new definitions. If you are any kind of leader, start leading prophetically right now!

Don't wait for everyone to understand and recognize titles. Titles mean almost nothing to revolutionaries. Don't wait for a full understanding of prophetic leadership before you begin acting prophetically. Act prophetically or you will never fully engage your destiny, never walk out your calling.

For the purposes of this book, I am not trying to clarify the distinctions of all five aspects of the ministry of Jesus, or the ascension gifts in all their complexities. A broad range of ideas is currently emerging because God is restoring foundational leadership.

Several international leaders have created excellent dialogue about the new apostolic reformation and provided compelling examples of its maturing and growth. I am simply saying here that all leaders, walking in any and every role of fivefold ministry must lead prophetically and prepare a people for the next season of revolutionary revival. Talking about an apostolic reformation is a first step to functioning in the restoration of these New Testament leadership roles, but fulfilling them is more about the people we lead than the leaders we are straining to identify as examples of apostles, prophets, and teachers. The best examples of apostolic reformation are leaders who are preparing a people ready to follow foundational leadership.

I remain a student of this reformation's development and growth. I will have more to say about it in future books about "David's Army" and "leaders who disciple cultures."

What I see here and now in the spirit and power of Elijah is about preparing a people ready to respond for the coming revolutionary revival. Prophetic leadership is essential to this revolution. A prophetic leadership is required and sent for this task. Until we prepare a people, the restoration of Jesus' ministry cannot properly function. Applying titles to conventional leadership will not move the Church into the next season. We will not experience fullness and fulfillment until we prepare a people for what is coming before it arrives.

An unusual authority and power is operating in this new leadership, and all leaders must measure their life's work by this new shift.

CONFRONTATION AND TRANSFORMATION

Prophetic leadership confronts. It is a work of hell to substitute perversions of destiny and purpose for what Jesus created. Prophetic leadership confronts the modern expressions of idolatry. Confrontation is absolutely necessary to prepare a people ready for divine visitation. This confrontation is one manifestation of the unusual spiritual authority and power of prophetic leadership that will confirm the prophetic voice.

Confrontation creates separation. It is not separation from as much as it is separation to. It is a natural consequence of confrontation that a remnant will be clarified among the crowd: the Church within the church will rise, separated to the next season.

The separation of a remnant will be, especially at first, painful and disruptive. Many people will be uncomfortable and will misidentify the spirit and power of Elijah because of the disruption and discomfort. It is a separation to something more than a separation from something.

The conventional church specializes in making people comfortable and creating situations in which disruption rarely occurs. The conventional church works very, very hard to create and maintain these levels of comfort and to protect people from disruptions. It is the inherent nature of "conventional," and basic to its success. Chapter One in the maintenance manual of *Church As Usual* bears the title "Keeping People Comfortable." It is basic to churches dominated by pastoral ministry more than prophetic leadership. (There is a difference between ministry and leadership.)

The spirit and power of Elijah challenges the religious norms and confronts the false comforts of conventional church. Jesus does not despise conventional church or He would not call it to revolutionary revival. Jesus does not wish to destroy the conventional church, or it would already be gone. Jesus merely ignores it because He only acknowledges activities that are "doing the will of the Father in Heaven." He is only aware of the anointable things.

Jesus is calling out to the conventional church, opening it to movements of revolution, but such a call is unavoidably confrontational and disruptive. It feels as if He is calling conventional church "from the outside."

To prepare a people for the Lord means transformation for people. Restoring means bringing back something lost. When it returns, what has been substituted in its place will be blown away like dust in a wind storm as if it had never been. It will be confrontational. It will be disruptive.

As If It Had Never Been...

In the vision I mentioned previously of Jesus standing up to claim His Church, I saw Him shake off the dust of centuries and the wind blew it away "as if it had never been." When revolutionary revival arrives, some things allowed to remain for a long time will be swept away as if they had never been.

Beware of the assumption that God likes things because He has left them alone! When the shaking comes, only God's foundations will stand sure!

When confrontation appears, it comes first to leaders. Leaders will shake and tremble. Leaders will be exposed for surgery. Leaders will be set apart for transformation. And, when the leaders are touched by the spirit and power of Elijah, some people will be unwilling to accept change and they will long for the former days of comfort, for their "old conventional pastor." When we see these transformed leaders standing up with unusual authority and power, we will be shocked by who they are and who they are not.

In the vision I had of Jesus claiming His Church in 2003, I heard Jesus say, "This is the day of opportunity. When the shaking comes, I will redistribute. Some will be raised and some lowered; some will be lifted and some destroyed. But in this time of shaking and redistribution, I will establish something you have never seen before in the earth. 'There will be a changing of the guard.' See, angels of the Lord are standing with swords in their hands—see, their hands are not empty!—but in their hands are great swords."

Jesus is lifting unlikely people from unlikely places to do unlikely things.

Endnote

1. See Deuteronomy 30:16, for example. The legal sense of judgment and opinions are unique from common usage. The more technical sense of God's judgments and opinions to which I refer here can be illustrated throughout Deuteronomy as Moses explains, applies, and executes the covenant culture of Israel. God's judgment decisions lay the foundation for His enactments, prescriptions, testimonies, and commandments. It is just as important to heed what God meant by His decisions as it is to hear and obey them. Americans have seen this

painfully illustrated in our culture as judgments rewritten with different opinions literally make the intent of our Constitution and court decisions mean the exact opposite of their initial intention. So, leaders must hear and execute the decisions of God with His opinions about them. An important resource would be the introduction to Deuteronomy in Everett Fox's excellent translation of the Torah, *The Five Books of Moses*, Schocken Books, New York, 1995, pages 841-848.

3

Unlikely People and Places

In the season of visitation, Jesus demands an accounting of His leaders. He measures their motivations and sentiments. He confronts sloppy or negligent commitments to His purposes—substituted human agendas, people-pleasing, or religious traditions. He requires transformation in His leaders because He demands change in His people.

Jesus will transform leaders. These transformed leaders, touched by His power, will pay a price with those unwilling to change, and the price will be taxing for some. Jesus will send leaders from outside the conventional church to confront the status quo inside it—a call from the outside, voices crying from wilderness obscurities.

To prepare a people for the Lord, for a visitation of Heaven, is no simple thing. The spirit and power of Elijah is about revolutionary revival and a restoration of something lost.

We have lost much of the ministry of Jesus, but He is restoring all of it, bringing His Church back to the days of the apostles when Jesus' ministry was fully functional and the fullness of the Spirit dominated the daily life of Christians. His first leaders came out of nowhere, nobodies whose leadership was undeniably the work of God, not man.

Personal Transformation

I am an example of a transformed existing leader. I began preaching when I was 15 years of age and ministered in conventional settings for more than 25 years, preaching against most of what I am and do now.

I preached that many gifts of the Spirit, whatever they might have been in New Testament times, were not operational and available here and now. I made fun of many of God's transformational leaders, leaders in healing, especially in Pentecostal and Charismatic circles, faith and word teachers, revivalists and prophets.

If someone had approached me and said, "In your forties, you will be touched by revival and you will operate in spiritual gifts, speak prophetic words, travel to other nations, and do what you have preached was false all these years," I would have certainly thought that person crazy! I would have said emphatically, "There ain't no way!"

However, I "knew" my 40th year would bring a big change. I knew I would begin to move into my life's work. Ruthanne and I moved to Florida that year, closer to the revival we would soon encounter. However, I was still a long way from transformational experiences.

After moving to Florida, I was teaching a seminar in Minnesota when a lady asked me where I lived. I replied, "Florida."

"Oh, then you know about the revival!" she said.

I was bewildered: "No, what revival?"

Unlikely People and Places

"The one in Pensacola."

Immediately my spirit knew I was going to that revival! The story is long, though interesting, about how God put Ruthanne and me in that revival—amazing, the trail of our preparatory experiences! However, one night soon after, "there we were," joining people who seemed strange, singing strange music, and experiencing God in strange ways.

At the close of that first service, we stood at the front for ministry. I had never been prayed for in the way they were praying for people, but I waited for the revival leaders to come and pray for me. They never came!

Finally, a teenage girl stood in front of me and gently placed her fingertips on my forehead. While she prayed, I fell down to the floor of the church...and God sat on me! Yes, God sat down on me, and I could not move. I could not lift my legs or arms. I could not wiggle my little finger! I could not open my eyelids! God was sitting on me!

I remember saying in my spirit, "Lord, what are you doing?"

He said, "You are so proud and arrogant, I cannot help you without knocking you out. Now, shut up and lie still while I fix you."

I had little choice because I had thoroughly surrendered, and by that time I was ready for radical change. I lay there on the floor for a long time. Transformation began.

Revival Leaders

Jesus is transforming existing leaders all over the world. He is interrupting their comfortable, conventional

The Spirit and Power of Elijah

lives with "suddenlies" of divine power and transformation. He is leading them through powerful preparatory experiences, leading them toward something they could never have dreamed or envisioned. He knows better than they what He wants and requires of their lives and leadership.

Their transformational experiences will not be exactly like mine or anyone else's, but they are intensely learning lessons of surrender. Their preparatory experiences lift them level by level into new places of spiritual change. They are giving their Isaacs to God. They are losing what they thought they had worked their whole lives to enjoy, trading conventional security for what seems wild, crazy, unusual, and unknown!

Sound familiar? Ready for revolution in your own life? To be ready for great awakening, you must experience personal awakening. Sound exciting? It certainly does to Ruthanne and me! Transformation changes everything; God starts with leaders, seeking to move on to the whole Church!

Revival comes through leaders. Revival continues with leaders. Revival spreads through leaders. The momentum of revival depends upon the preparation, transformation, and release of new leaders, or it is limited to and dies with the leaders who originated it.

Whatever revival is, it will become something else or cease to be true revival unless it perpetuates itself in new revival leaders. Revival is all about leaders. Revival leaders are transformational leaders. They are personally transformed, and they lead others into personal transformation. Whatever we customarily title this process, it should become our operative definition of "discipling."

Unlikely People and Places

Revival leaders must first encounter God in personal, preparatory experiences. These encounters are always intense and transformational. Nearly every great prophetic leader God used to bring revival has had an experience with God in which he said, "Lord, if you don't stop or strengthen me, I will die in this manifestation of glory."

Ruthanne and I recently met with a revival leader who led the church where we first encountered the glory. We were deeply touched to see continuing hunger for God's glory in him and his wife. He said, "Once you've been in His glory, nothing else can ever satisfy." They had been in a manifestation of Glory that was intense and transformational. Their encounter with Glory changed everything.

Transformational Leaders

There is a transformational aspect to the glory. (See Paul's revelation about glory in Second Corinthians 3:16-18.) Glory encounters are available to us in the new covenant. The revealing of the Lord's glory releases spiritual change. Transformation and prophetic leadership operate together.

Transformational leadership is discipling leadership, the leadership that best fits and fulfills the mission of the Church. Jesus is redefining "discipling," restoring its original essence to the Church. Leadership that comforts people, pleases people, entertains people, claims and uses people is not true discipling leadership.

Conventional church has often failed to bring personal transformation because it has not brought true discipling. Conventional church leadership has not led God's people into personal maturity for the same reason. Today's conventional church is failing in the arena of cultural transformation because it is failing to release personal transformation. That is about to change!

Repentance was a keynote of John the Baptist's ministry and the spirit and power of Elijah. It is fundamental to revolutionary revival. To get ready means to change. Repentance releases the grace of transformation because it appropriates the power of the Cross. Repentance is more than confessing bad behavior; it is spiritual change that transforms behavior.

For revolutionary revival to begin, spread, and flourish, something spiritual must be changed within God's people, and something transformational must be released into their spirits. For revolutionary revival to touch a city, something spiritual must change over that city, and something transformational must be released within its culture.

Jesus uses confrontation to initiate and complete transformation. Prophetic leaders are confrontational, and their continuous involvement is essential to building and maintaining the spiritual momentum of revolutionary revival.

The spirit and power of Elijah handed off to Jesus from John reaches fulfillment in Jesus' ministry. He operated in it and integrated it into His ministry. Jesus then passed His ministry to His Church. The ministry of Jesus is a discipling, transformational leadership ministry sent into the earth to transform every culture impacted by its prophetic leadership.

Unlikely People and Places

Receive confrontation when the prophetic leaders Jesus sends push you to change. Your preparation demands change. You are not ready for God's visitation. If you were ready, no forerunner would be necessary. If you were ready, no transformational experience would be needed.

Revolutionary revival leaders will be confrontational. Repentance will be evident and widespread wherever the spirit and power of Elijah is at work.

Change made by natural means, without this spiritual operation, will be short-lived and shallow. We cannot create the needed change with human programs, doctrinal principles, cameo personalities, or delivery-packaged purposes.

Revolutionary revival means existing leaders will be transformed as Jesus invades the Church to capture and claim its leaders. The next class of leaders will be people who seem to "come out of nowhere" who lead mini-movements of radical change.

Revolutionary revival means emerging leaders will be transformed as Jesus invades the places conventional church has written off. The next class of leaders will bridge spiritual changes inside conventional church with spiritual changes from outside.

Jesus is bringing the disenfranchised into places of leadership preparation much as David's army was assembled in his wilderness obscurity. Jesus is capturing and claiming leaders who have few apparent qualifications. Jesus is teaching conventional church that their ministry methods, doctrinal definitions, and leadership validations are just too small for the next season!

God Uses All People

Elijah's origins are mysterious at best. Even though we have some excellent information in Scripture, we are really pressed to know how to identify a "Tishbite!"

"Elijah the Tishbite of Tishbe in Gilead" doesn't really tell us a lot. There is some precedent that *Tishbite* means "stranger," and the verse would read "Elijah the stranger from among the strangers in Gilead." (See 1 Kings 17:1.) Elijah may have migrated as a settler into the desert to the east of Jericho from which John the Baptist came centuries later. Either way, Elijah is not from Jerusalem, not from "headquarters," nor identified with any known prophetic school or movement. The implication is clear—Elijah is not one of the in-crowd. He is an outsider, an ordinary man called to do a godly task.

This is precisely the way things are happening in our generation. The leaders of the new are not necessarily the ones we would have expected. The voices and words are new, the inflections and speech patterns are new. God is at it again—unlikely people are doing unlikely things in unlikely places.

Ordinary Leaders—Everywhere!

The new worship leaders are not on the short list of those with "amazing abilities." They are people unlikely to become prophetic worship leaders. Some are elevated from seed beds expertly planted by professional promotion to produce fame and fortune; others emerge from places of silence in unexpected ways.

One of my favorite intercession and worship CDs was produced in a bedroom clothes closet! My friend purchased

Unlikely People and Places

simple equipment and crawled behind the clothes to record sessions of instrumental worship. It's awesome!

Other unknown worship leaders are emerging from hidden places, secret chambers of preparation, unseen, taking the Church into the next wave of worship. They are "coming in from their wildernesses" like Elijah, David, John, and Jesus came from beyond the Jordan. A new sound of worship with a fully developed spirit suddenly appears.

This is but one example of the "unlikely people" scenario of which God seems fond. He selects passed over people. He has a grasp of the facts beyond those available to human reason. His measure of "potential" uses a very different yardstick, a different system of measurement. One leader says, "If I had the last twenty years to do over, I would invest my leadership more in passion than potential." Jesus seems to be investing more in passion than potential in these days!

God's mainstream isn't always the same as our mainstream. Jesus is much bigger than any one aspect of His Kingdom. He chooses leaders who seem to appear "out of nowhere" to confront the Body with His agenda. But they seem perfectly normal to Jesus! We say they are not part of the mainstream, but they are in God's mainstream.

Elijah was "a Tishbite"—whatever that is. He was probably from Tishbe—wherever that is. His father was not famous. His mother had no pedigree. He didn't attend the best schools of the prophets or come from the fastest growing segment of God's work. He was not chosen by the king or appointed by any man. He was an ordinary person called to shut up the heavens and speak to a nation;

an ordinary man was to build an altar in the name of the Lord.

God's intention in the time of Ahab's reign makes Elijah appear an unlikely candidate for prophetic leadership. Baal worship is funded and honored by Jezebel, who kills prophets, babies, and enslaves a nation's men with manipulation and intimidation. Elijah is not a politically astute representative, not a good ambassador to the court, a man untrained in the proper enunciation of diplomacy.

The numbers don't make Elijah's goals seem feasible either. One unknown prophetic leader against 850 false prophetic leaders who have the backing of the queen, confronting a whole nation on a mountain far removed from the centers of commerce and culture with a rather ridiculous notion about fire falling from Heaven. No, this seemed to be a disaster just waiting to happen. Only three years of intense drought could make Ahab desperate enough to talk about such a meeting. (See 1 Kings 18.)

JOHN AND DAVID

We see the same element of the ridiculous in John the Baptist. His ministry certainly defies reason, which is standard procedure with the spirit and power of Elijah.

John is born to parents well beyond the best years of childbearing with no previous experience rearing children. No human logic exists for John's parents to have a destiny child. Nothing in their present or past condition puts them on the "A list" of good candidates to adopt, much less support the notion that this woman should produce a son herself at her advanced age.

Unlikely People and Places

After the glorious and miraculous birthing, John disappears (from the Scriptures) and shows up later in strange clothes eating strange food, crying out in the wilderness. Instead of renting a local synagogue or using a town square for his meetings, he wants to baptize people in the Jordan River. Instead of the specially built mikvah baths prepared by the orthodoxy, John wants to do something nobody had ever done!

Jesus is sending leaders whose look and methods don't fit. The people God is raising and releasing in the spirit and power of Elijah look like David's misfit mighty men. The disenfranchised living in debt, despair, and discouragement gathered to David's wilderness where he became their leader in exile.

God gave David his mighty men before he became king; this is the pattern we are seeing today. The greatest release of apostolic and prophetic leadership comes through years of developmental discipling. While it seems to appear suddenly, the preparation process is arduous.

Folks pushed out and pushed aside, who don't seem to fit the present program, but carry an anointed passion that nearly consumes them, are becoming leaders "suddenly set in place." We say, "These leaders are coming out of nowhere!" However, they came from somewhere and are going somewhere; they were born and raised with the stuff of destiny and are now being released to fly with the eagles!

How do we recognize these new prophetic leaders? We cannot use our present stereotypes, and we cannot look exclusively inside conventional church. They are young and old, male and female, and they represent every race under Heaven. Most do not fit modernized models of professional clergy. Who are these prophetic leaders, these unlikely people from unlikely places daring to do unlikely things?

4

Today's Prophetic Leaders

If you had told me at any time in my first 40 years of life or the first 25 years of ministry I would be doing, saying, ministering, or experiencing what I am now, I would have instantly, definitely, and emphatically graded your revelation insight as "dim and fading fast!" Nothing in my previous training, birth and education, religious experience and ministry remotely hinted I would be who I am or do what I am now doing. I was an existing leader who became transformed to help prepare God's people for the next level.

In his day, Elijah was an emerging leader arriving from outside with unusual spiritual authority and power to prepare God's people for the next wave. Unknowns without proper pedigrees for credibility are being used to lead the Church today. Today's prophetic leaders are both existing and emerging leaders.

Unlikely leaders are coming out of "their wildernesses" broken and leaning on the arm of the Lord! All over the world, leaders of every kind in every place are hearing a still small voice. They are hungry and thirsty for something more. These existing leaders are being transformed by unusual spiritual authority and power and equipped with unusual spiritual authority and power to take the Church to another level. They sense something is coming, or more importantly, Someone is coming and they must prepare a people for Him and lead in the spirit and power of Elijah.

Maybe you are such an existing or emerging prophetic leader yourself! Be assured—you are not alone. You have friends! You have fellow Tishbites, strangers coming up from the desert with a fire burning in their bones. God is touching many unlikely leaders for this great end-time revival harvest. You too may be called to operate in the spirit and power of Elijah!

Prophetic Leadership in the New Testament Church

Prophecy is about fulfillment, and prophetic leaders are responsible for declaring and enforcing God's decisions. Nothing but full execution of Father's "season strategy" will do. Good efforts, good beginnings are not obedience. We must get God what He wants.

In the beginning of the Church, prophetic leaders began well, preparing the Body for Father's season strategy, manifesting the life of Jesus in demonstrations of power, attracting thousands into the kingdom, and creating a new spiritual generation of leaders like Stephen. Prophetic leaders prepared the people for extending the Church into Samaria and the ends of the earth, the "what God wanted" part of Jesus' instructions concerning the power they would receive in the Upper Room.

Dramatic prophetic experiences awakened Peter to preach to Gentiles, and Paul a fuller revelation of

Father's purposes for the nations. Early prophetic leadership in the Church remained focused upon Jerusalem until persecution moved the centers of Christianity to Damascus and finally to Ephesus toward the later years of the first century.

God wanted a powerful, glorious Church who ministered by the power, gifts, and operations of Holy Spirit. He wanted leaders who could bring healing, deliverance, and redemption to individuals of every kind, age, gender, and social standing. He wanted an international Church of all nations. He wanted expressions of the Church in every nation, city by city, a localized rebuilding of David's tent of meeting. He wanted His purpose declared to kings, governors, and emperors. He wanted to extend His kingdom worldwide, to take over the world with spiritual leaders! He wanted prophetic leaders who could deliver His Gospel with power and authority and turn reborn people into kingdom people equipped to make more prophetic leaders themselves. We can see what God wanted these prophetic leaders to get for Him in the leadership Jesus designed for His Church.

The prophet, priest, and king roles were fulfilled in Jesus, as the Son of David, for it was David who executed judgment in his kingdom as a type of Jesus' new covenant. Jesus arrived to establish the worldwide, everlasting Kingdom covenant and culture that David founded in Israel. Both David and Jesus *functioned* in all three governing aspects God designed for His people, but Jesus *fulfilled* all three.

Paul says the three governing aspects of Jesus' ministry are apostles, prophets, and teachers; these three are the first, second, and third aspects of governing in the Body of Christ. God has appointed in the church first of all apostles, second prophets, third teachers. (See 1 Corinthians 12:28.)

It is what these leaders do that defines their roles because the terms were specifically chosen to reflect how Jesus brought these roles into His Kingdom and defined them for function within His Church. His Kingdom is more than His Church, and Kingdom leaders define leadership functions He designed for the Church.

In short, I believe that all New Testament Church leaders must be prophetic leaders. They must lead prophetically. Especially in this season of revolutionary revival, all leadership in the Body must accurately anticipate the next season and prepare the whole Church to walk in the fullness and fulfillment of that season's purpose. Prophetic leaders should be focused upon people because New Testament Church leaders equip people to do ministry.

Something is happening in "church" right now that demands an immediate response. Tens of thousands are moving away while at the same time crying out for new leaders, demanding a more authentic definition of *church*. A new leadership must step into the vacuum left by the inadequacy of conventional leadership, a leadership that will answer Jesus' call for revolutionary revival and historic harvest.

Unless conventional church leaders immediately move into a more prophetic mode, it may be too late to salvage much of the conventional for the next season. It will exist as an old, empty wineskin. It will remain, to be sure, but more as a museum of past moves of God than a force for what is coming next.

Analytical study confirms what I am saying through prophetic insight. A total reshaping of the Body is happening that is redefining leadership and ministry. Conventional church as it is will be much, much too small to accommodate God's strategy in the next season.

If existing leaders are not personally transformed to lead people into the new season, they will be in danger of fighting against God to preserve what should be emptied out and protect what needs no protection.

It is all about the leadership: prophetic leaders preparing a prophetic people. The whole structure must be reshaped and retooled and reprioritized to accommodate the next season.

While most American churches are still fiddling with programs that have run their courses, playing "catch up" with last season's trends, Jesus is calling them to prepare a people ready to respond to the next season. The call of God for a Kingdom people demands that we begin to lead as prophetic leaders.

The conventional church leadership model is too small for what is happening, and the Church must immediately release and function in a new leadership. That leadership must be prophetic at every level.

The Elijah mantle prepares a people for the Lord, so people are his focus. Elijah told Ahab to call the people to Mount Carmel, not just Ahab. Elijah was after God's people because God was after His people. (See 1 Kings 18:20.)

Prepare the Lord a People

When the apostle John saw the Revelation of Jesus Christ, he saw Jesus walking with "the churches," real churches and real cities of ancient Asia Minor. In that revelation moment, seeing the Head of the Church in prophetic vision, John saw fire in Jesus' eyes. (See Revelation 1:14.)

The fire in Jesus' eyes is His passionate love for what is His, what He bought and paid for, what His death and resurrection secured for His Kingdom. The passion of Jesus burns for His Church. The passion of Jesus is His passion for His Father's will to be done, for the Father to get what the Father wants.

I have seen that fire. John saw it in prophetic vision. More than just seeing it, he experienced the passion that fire represents. I have experienced that fiery passion. When you experience the passion of Jesus, you are experiencing the passionate heart of the Father! You will begin to experience what Father feels for what is His and for what He wants. His passionate love burns hot! It will overwhelm you and transform the way you see yourself, your destiny, and His Church.

Prophetic leaders are all about what Father wants. Prophecy accurately anticipates what is coming next, not just anything or everything that is coming next, but what is coming next from the Father's heart.

The Father is in charge of times and seasons and Jesus empowers His Church for His Father's will. So, the fire in His eyes is not for His own desire. Jesus is out to get Father what Father wants.

The prophetic leader's eyes must burn with the passion of the Father. The fire that burns in Jesus' eyes is His prophetic vision, and it measures "what is" by "what is coming next" from the Father's heart.

Prophetic leadership will move the whole Church closer to Father's heart because pure prophetic passion is fueled by what Father wants. In Jesus, we can experience passion perfectly focused upon the will of the Father. With prophetic leadership, we can move the whole Church into focused passion to get Father what He wants.

For Jesus' leadership to be expressed in His Church, the leaders must have His burning vision and passion for the Father's will to be done.

For the Lord, Not Ourselves

The spirit and power of Elijah prepares a people for the Lord. Not for ourselves. Not for any earthly agenda. Not for men or human institutions. This Elijah mantle is all about Jesus leading a people ready to receive and exercise Kingdom dominion. Preparing people for ourselves does more than dilute their commitment to Kingdom priorities; it distances them from spiritual reality by substituting our leadership for Jesus' leadership.

God's people belong to God. The coming revolutionary revival will reclaim for Jesus what is His. It will redefine and recalibrate Church leadership, restoring leadership roles to the Body. During the restoration of apostles, prophets, and teachers to the Body, much of the emphasis has been upon the validity of these leaders, but the greatest or highest expression of the restoration will be realized when it involves Jesus more intimately in leading His people.

While it is true that this restoration releases men and women who operate in unusual spiritual authority and power, the restoration is not designed to consolidate or concentrate leadership in men. This restoration of unusually authoritative and powerful leaders will concentrate and consolidate the leadership of Jesus.

The people of John's day were a people prepared for many social, religious, and political agendas. The entire culture of Israel was designed to function as a Kingdom culture with little separation between sacred and secular things. Israel's leaders had pirated that designed intention to fulfill their own purposes. The temple system had been corrupted by human power for political purpose. The legal system had been corrupted by human compromise for personal profit. The political system had been corrupted by human ambition for building coalitions. The people had been prepared for men, not God.

John was sent with Elijah's mantle to confront these false claims. It was the same authority and power that confronted the religious spirits of Jezebel, the system that used God's people for earthly purposes.

Idolatry is simply substituting something for God, and the church can be as guilty of providing substitutes for the work, worship, and will of God as witches. Idolatry substitutes the voice of man for the voice of God, and the church can be as guilty of killing prophets as Jezebel.

How easily we cut and paste symbols and labels from Jesus' ministry to imitate Him, and use these Christian totems to validate our own ideas. How comfortable religion becomes a bronze serpent source-and-resource substitute for the Cross!

Beware the tendency to worship God's instruments and tools instead of or more than God Himself. Beware the tendency to use God or attempt to obligate Him to fulfill your own agendas. Beware the modern pandemic of using God's people by preparing them to follow you and fulfill your vision-casting.

When the spirit and power of Elijah functions in any culture, the conventional church feels an immediate challenge to its program, personalities, principles, and purposes.

Program-oriented churches are dying away; all programs have limited lifespan. Personality-oriented churches can only reach as far as and live as long as the personality upon which they are built; personality is not enough. Principle-oriented churches have the narrow focus of their principles; they only exist to preserve and protect principles that need no preservation or protection. Purpose-oriented churches that substitute earthly vision for God's purpose only limit church vision to man-measured fulfillment; they create cycles instead of fulfilling purposes.

Each of these forms of church has restored an element of Kingdom building to the whole Body. The prophetic concepts do not fit well in old wineskin institutions, and the essence of revelation they restored is usually lost because churchanity attempts to use God, His people, and His ideas to fulfill their own purposes.

Presence-oriented churches operate in the reality of Father's passion for His purposes. Jesus has a fiery passion for His Church. You don't want to get in His way right now! He has come to claim His Church and prophetic leadership is arising to get us ready for a fresh falling of that fire!

It's About Inheritance

In his prophetic announcement of John the Baptist's birth, archangel Gabriel clearly states the function and purpose of the spirit and power of Elijah operating in his life. He describes the operational characteristics of a prophetic leader anointed with Elijah's mantle.

The angel begins with Malachi's prophecy of Elijah's coming and expands to a fuller revelation of prophetic leadership.

The angel says, "He will be mighty in the Lord's presence. He will never drink wine or any strong drink, for he will be filled with Holy Spirit before he is born. He will return many Israelites to the Lord their God." (See Luke 1:15.)

Before Jesus arrives, John arrives in the spirit and power of Elijah to restore the generations, persuade those not yet persuaded of righteous wisdom, and to prepare a people ready for the Lord when He arrives.

A prophetic leader is set apart in particular ways that move him under the protective arm of God—his greatness is never more apparent than when he is in God's presence. "He will be mighty in the Lord's presence." Or, the strength of his life and ministry will be Presence-driven. Because he will be full of the Holy Spirit from the beginning, he will live a life empowered by God's manifested presence.

His lifestyle is set apart in particular ways that move him close to God's beating heart: he abstains from that which dilutes his awareness of reality and truth. "He will never drink wine or strong drink." The call of God separates prophetic leaders and people to a lifestyle of intimacy with God. More than separating them *from* anything, it separates them *to* something that displaces everything else that dilutes their awareness of God.

John's ministry says, "Something lost is coming back. Some people astray are coming home."

His function in preparing a way for the Lord is to get God's people ready for a divine appointment: he is assigned to a people destined to receive a heavenly visit. "He will return many Israelites to the Lord their God."

John's ministry restores something lost. The prophetic leader reunites the generations so the preserved purpose of God may be released for fullness and fulfillment in a faithful generation—he restores the hearts to release the inheritance of generations. "He will arrive before the Lord to restore the generations."

As a prophetic leader, you will have revelation recognition of what the people you lead were created to be and called to do. The success of your leadership will be measured by how well they fulfill their destinies. As a prophetic person, you must be transformed because your self-image is the greatest limiting factor to the fulfillment of your own destiny. As a prophetic leader, you must bring transformation to others because their greatest limiting factor is false self-image.

You were created to be and called to do, and all this connects with your natural and spiritual generations. You were not born in a vacuum, but were a continuation of a purpose which you can be empowered to fulfill.

Something left undone comes to you from your natural and spiritual generations, but without prophetic leadership you will never even know its there, let alone fulfill it. There's more in you than you know.

Only Jesus knows what's in you. What you've inherited is not obvious to you or anyone else except by spiritual revelation. That's how Jesus communicates destiny. Prophetic leadership helps you to become all He created you to be and do all He called you to do. Many times God reveals to you through your leaders what He alone knows of your destiny.

Prophetic leaders and people must be restored inside-out, heart-to-heart with God and their spiritual generations. "He will restore the hearts...." Inheritance is at stake. Prophetic leadership is about fulfilling what's always been available. God is calling you to walk in the fullness and fulfillment of that inheritance.

This is the sense of father's hearts and children's hearts. Jesus says the thief only arrives to steal, kill, and destroy. The spirit and power of Elijah restores the generations, reattaches the flow of purpose and resurrects what the thief has murdered.

Prophetic leadership prepares a prophetic people—a people prepared to fulfill and implement previously prophesied purposes. Prophetic leaders prepare a people to be ready for the Lord when the Lord arrives in a season of fulfillment; and the success of their leadership will be apparent when God's remnant is prepared to receive His visitation.

You are being prepared! You are being called to help prepare others for the next season. That's why you are reading this book. You are searching, crying out, pressing in, and looking forward; you know there must be something more!

5

Prepare the Lord a People

Preparing Prophetic People

Only a prophetic people can truly discern the wind of the Spirit. The aroma and fire of the spirit and power of Elijah released now into the spiritual atmosphere is more evidence that God is about to do something. Before He does, He provides a period of preparation. He opens ears and eyes. He sends leaders with special anointing and ministry who have the spirit and power to restore and prepare.

The spirit and power of Elijah prepares a people ready to receive the Lord. That's the point of the preparation—we will recognize Jesus! We will recognize the truth because we are prepared.

Elijah spoke prophetic words, completed prophetic acts, and fulfilled prophetic instructions. Prophetic people respond best to prophetic leadership when they discern the validity of the prophetic mantle. Prophetic people stay in step with the forward progress that prophetic leadership maintains.

Although prophetic leaders and people learn the valuable lessons of "waiting on the Lord," they advance more rapidly than others because they see and hear what God is doing and where God is going. Leaders are bold when they are prophetically prepared.

WHEN YOU KNOW WHERE TO GO,
YOU CAN GET THERE MORE QUICKLY.

Prophetic leaders seem unusual to us if we lack a prophetic insight, but they appear normal to God and prophetic people. They appear off-beat and out of step to those seeing and hearing with natural eyes and ears! This is the sense of the charge of the Revelation: "He that has ears to hear, hear what the Spirit says to the churches!"

God sends unusual representatives. God calls and uses unlikely people. Prophetic people know God chooses unusual leaders to do unusual things, often misunderstood until their obedience unveils His greater purpose.

PREPARING THE REMNANT

Prophecy is about fulfillment, and prophetic leaders lead people into fullness. That fullness and fulfillment must touch individuals *within* the Church in order to release fullness and fulfillment *through* the Church. That fullness and fulfillment must restore purpose and destiny, and must declare and enforce God's revelation decisions with unusual authority and power.

Since God has released the spirit and power of Elijah in this generation, we know God is coming for a visit! God appoints the spirit and power of Elijah to the season before He visits His people, a time when God's people must be awakened and made ready for Him.

This was Elijah's task. He was a prophetic leader of restoration sent during a season of hope, a time in which God dealt with Israel to restore her purpose and destiny. In other words, God sent Elijah to minister to Israel in a way that would restore the nation. All He called the nation to be and do was still available for full restoration, preserved and reserved for fulfillment by an obedient generation.

Paul says, "God did not thrust away His people whom He foreknew. Do you not know what the Scripture says, how Elijah pleads with God against Israel saying: 'Lord, they killed your prophets. They drug down your altars, and I alone am left, and they seek to kill me?' And what is the Divine answer to him? 'I have reserved to myself seven thousand who have not bowed their knees to Baal.' So also in the present time a remnant has been established according to the selection of God's gracious love." (See 1 Kings 19.)

It is interesting to note the important words of this New Testament Elijah discussion: *remnant*, *reserved*, and *in the present time*. Paul says God is working in his generation as He had worked in Elijah's day—He chooses a remnant in the present time and reserves them for Himself. Paul says, "God is working with the spirit and power of Elijah in my generation to prepare a remnant selected to fulfill His purposes." (See Romans 11.)

Right now the nations are pulsing with new prophetic leadership that calls God's people to a season of restoration and transformation. We should be looking for transformational leaders with authority and responsibility to confront whole cultures. These are prophetic leaders who function to bring transformation to individuals and leaders. At every level, God is giving us a new prophetic leadership.

Elijah Restores All

As Jesus stood on a mountain with three of His leading disciples, Father pulled back the "natural curtain" to reveal the spiritual reality. The three men saw the glory within Jesus, the glory of His Kingdom. Jesus had prophesied this encounter the week before it happened:

Some of you will not taste death until you see the Son of Man arrive in the glory of His Kingdom. Six days later, Jesus takes Peter, James, and John up on a mountain with Him…and Jesus is transformed before their eyes. In that moment, Jesus talks with law and prophets—Moses and Elijah—and the glory of His Kingdom is revealed.

At that moment, the glory of His Kingdom was revealed, not created. It was already real, already present, already spiritual reality. Father revealed the nature of the Kingdom to glorify His Son. Then Jesus tells His disciples the spirit and power of Elijah has visited their generation "to restore all."

Coming down from the mountain, Jesus enjoined them, saying, "Tell no one the vision until the Son of Man is raised from the dead." His followers questioned him, "Why then do the scribes say that Elijah must come first?" And he answered, "Elijah indeed comes and will restore all." (See Matthew 16:1-13.)

The disciples understand that Jesus is speaking of John the Baptist, that Israel has rejected the preparation ministry of John. Jesus is speaking of Elijah to clarify what this anointing does in a nation marked for awakening and harvest—it restores all.

The spirit and power of Elijah represents God's work to prepare a people to fulfill their redemptive purpose. He restores something lost, brings back something missing. Jesus restores what is necessary to release revolutionary revival, and restores what is necessary to fulfill any people's redemptive purpose.

Every culture has a redemptive purpose that naturally establishes God's Kingdom in the earth. Each culture brings something unique to the whole Kingdom of God that is essential, something God designed that culture to provide for the whole Kingdom.

The work of hell is to destroy, steal, and kill God's purpose for His people, and the most obvious work of hell in any culture is probably the best example of a perversion of its redemptive purpose. In other words, the very thing most hellish about a culture may represent hell's perversion of its unique purpose, its contribution to the Kingdom.

If a nation's music is corrupted, the worship sound has probably been perverted in order to frustrate and destroy that redemptive purpose. If the nation's economy suffers injustice and graft, their economic strength is probably one Kingdom purpose of that culture. If the children are exploited and rejected, that culture is set to release sons and daughters as Kingdom leaders and representatives into the nations.

Revival Nations

Brazil is a revival nation. The passion of Brazil has been perverted to celebrate the works of hell. False religions and witchcraft have perverted God's purposes for this people. Yet, the music and dance so powerfully exhibited in carnival represents a perversion of the true redemptive purpose of this culture.

Today, we are seeing a mighty release of prophetic leadership in revival nations during this generation, and Brazil is a leading revival nation. The spirit and power of Elijah operates there to restore Brazil's redemptive purposes. God brought together in Brazil aspects of several distant cultures. He preserved and reserved these elements for a future fulfillment in a faithful Brazilian generation.

God preserved a unique sound from several European and African cultures. One of Brazil's purposes is worship, and God has been busy restoring His sound, His music, His worship, His dance, His celebration, and His passion to a generation of Brazilians! It is a new sound, a new song, a new dance to be seen and heard around the world! This is the spirit and power of Elijah preparing a people for the Lord! Brazil is a nation poised to impact nations in the early years of this new millennium as Brazilian fire burns on every continent.

Revival Movements in the United States

Another excellent example of the spirit and power of Elijah may be seen in America's "The Call" youth movement. What began as events will begin again as a revolutionary revival movement aimed at young people called to be a generation of prophetic leaders. Jesus is giving this generation prophetic leadership, and mantles that rest upon today's prophetic leaders are available for transition.

"Promises Keepers" brought men together for a prophetic purpose and broke through countless barriers that separated American Christians, helping to forge a more united spiritual front against the complete secularization of our culture. "The Call" movement is helping create a similar spiritual infrastructure for revolutionary revival.

Promise Keepers brought men into new freedom in worship and prayer; now, numerous movements on a smaller scale are similarly rising in America inside and outside every flavor of church in every region of the nation. These are examples of prophetic leadership spawning mini-movements of revolutionary revival.

It is no longer a question of "will God visit America?" but whether or not God's people will be ready to receive Him when He arrives. Unless conventional church leaders begin to lead prophetically, moving toward transformation and embracing "what is coming next" for the Body soon, the prophetic leadership movements will create a prophetic remnant outside conventional church as a foundation for the next season of America's Christian faith.

God is preparing a people ready to respond to His visitation to the United States. I believe six previous waves of renewal have come to America in varying levels of spiritual intensity and impact in terms of population and purpose. Revolutionary revival has begun in America in preparation for another wave of Awakening. During the centennial of the Azusa Street Mission outpouring in 1906, we were especially consciousness that Jesus can release new wine and unusual spiritual authority and power as Father introduces a new season with new strategies for Kingdom building.

A new prophetic leadership is arising in America inside and outside conventional church, a prophetic leadership that Jesus is sending to prepare a people for the Lord before this next wave of revival. The level of acceptance for this prophetic leadership will set the level of acceptance for the awakening that is coming. As the acceptance of John the Baptist set the baseline for the acceptance of Jesus, America is making her decisions for the next season by her acceptance of today's new prophetic leaders.

God is releasing the mantle of Elijah in many cultures to accomplish redemptive restorations! The church's mission is to "disciple cultures," and only transformation can restore and fulfill redemptive purposes God has preserved in these cultures.

God is not leaving the United States out of this international restoration movement. He is sending transformational leaders to America. He has not given up on this nation!

A large, pervasive expression of revolutionary revival is becoming obvious—Jesus is creating a rumbling discontent in millions of American believers. A new breed of revolutionaries are being called who are intent upon "living Christian" more than merely identifying with a church, revolutionaries of every age interested in something more than conventional "churchanity."

This revolution is too far advanced to stop—it represents both the greatest opportunity and most urgent demand for new leadership in modern Christian history.

Father gives people the leadership they deserve, and Holy Spirit is creating this groundswell of holy discontent. Jesus' strategy for the multiple, grassroots mini-movements will feed the momentum of this revolutionary revival. These mini-movements require tens of thousands of new prophetic leaders. These new leaders will prepare millions of America's disenfranchised believers for the next wave of spiritual awakening.

George Barna of the Barna Research Group says America holds an ever-increasing number of revolutionaries. He says these are devout followers of Jesus Christ serious about living their faith, and living Christ-centered lives. Some of them have conventional church connections, but millions do not because they are no longer identifiable by local church affiliations and flavors. Their spiritual life cannot be categorized by answering the question, "Where do you attend church?" This is not to be interpreted as anti-church as much as it is prophetic anticipation.

These revolutionaries are, in contrast, truly committed to Christian living 24-7, defining spiritual life by being the Church more than attending one. He notes that this is creating the greatest revolution in American Christian history.[1]

The Fullness of the Church

Paul says Jesus is far above every ruler, authority, power, dominion, and every name, that Father has put everything under Jesus' feet and made Him Head of everything for the good of the Church. He says the Church is Jesus' Body. (See Ephesians 1:20-23.)

Then Paul says that the Church is the fullness of the One who fills everything in every way. Fullness and fulfillment come through Jesus, but Jesus is restoring fullness and bringing fulfillment through His Church. Jesus is restoring the fullness of the Church by the fullness of the Spirit in the fullness of time! Jesus is visiting His Church to make it glorious, claiming and restoring His Church. (See 2 Corinthians 3:8 and Ephesians 5:27.)

The manmade and artificial has run its course. The substitutes are fading. The Lamb has come and He is blowing away the modern idolatry of human principle, personality, program, and purpose like dust in the wind.

Don't get in His way! Jesus has come to make a claim on His people. He wants them prepared for the Lord, not prepared for anyone or anything else! He is realizing full restoration in His Church, leading a long parade of transformed people into glory to provide a means of restoring all to His Father's will.

Full Restoration

Jesus is preparing His Church for a full restoration of the Ministry of Jesus, the Mandate of Transformational Discipling, and the Mission of Discipling Cultures.

While we have seen tremendous harvest in recent history, especially during the last century since the Azusa Street Revival, we still are not seeing transformational leadership necessary for discipling cultures. While we are building bigger organizations and accumulating more believers, we remain generally irrelevant to our cultures, and the world is comfortable simply ignoring us.

The ministry of the Church is the ministry of Jesus. He established ministry, defined ministry, performed and fulfilled ministry, and gave this ministry to His Body.

The mandate for discipling is personal and cultural transformation. Jesus established discipling as the basis for leadership development and Kingdom citizenship. He turned ordinary people into extraordinary leaders. This is true discipleship.

The mission of the Church is more than getting people saved and accumulating believers. We are commissioned to transform ordinary individuals into ministering champions and transform entire cultures by confronting them with truth and power, establishing the Kingdom of God. Jesus intends to take over the world by discipling cultures, and He commissioned the Church to represent Him in this purpose.

Jesus is bringing something back that the Church has lost. Something that "faded out" after the first century is "fading back in" in the last days! Maybe the most important element of the operation is that Jesus is doing this work, not us.

This changes everything! He is not willing to leave anyone out! He is sending prophetic leaders, banging on doors, upsetting apple carts, shaking foundations, and calling us to revolutionary revival.

Foundations for Restoration

Not all leaders are prophets; but they all need to lead prophetically. Some of them are prophets; but all the leaders of revolutionary revival are foundational. They are laying new foundations under the Church, the spiritual infrastructure of revolutionary revival. They have a wide variety of personalities, callings, and ministries, and cannot be pigeon-holed into some ecclesiastical category. However, they all operate in the spirit and power of Elijah preparing a people ready for the Lord.

These leaders are unique. Their leadership redefines words like *church*, *missionary*, *ministry*, *leader*, and *mission*. They are men and women in the "grip of God" who have little choice but to walk out what God has put within them. They must obey or die. Their only option is the release of Father's burning passion for His purposes, men and women paying a price for being different, demanding a different outcome, and creating a different result.

PREPARATIONAL LEADERS

All preparational leaders have a distinguishing demonstration of their leadership—they are *transformational* leaders. They have been personally transformed by an unusual spirit and power. They transform other leaders with unusual spirit and power. They make transformed leaders who make other transformational leaders. They are out to change everyone and everything with an unusual spiritual authority and power!

Preparational leaders are transformational because transformation is God's way of preparing His people. Redemption is transformational and the Church's ministry is transformational. It is Jesus' ministry.

The restoration of the Church must be transformational. Preparation is intrinsically transformational. The Church must be filled with individually transformed people, led by individually transformed leaders, and must minister transformation to the next spiritual generations.

A new leadership paradigm is emerging in the Church everywhere at the same time, in nations worldwide. It may originate in cultures from which the Church has not previously expected new leadership to arise, for a new leadership is coming that redefines commonly understood words and concepts. The new leadership expands our definitions.

Prophetic leaders can only successfully lead when they lead prophetic people. Something released through them must backwash to them from the people who walk in their leadership.

The small groups movement has helped us anticipate the next season, and each of the myriad forms has demanded change; yet the present state of small groups is not its ultimate expression. Much of the prophetic purposes of mini-movements in the previous generation have been force-fit into conventional church, a practice that diminishes their momentum for revolutionary revival.

Small groups have helped restore leadership, discipling, and the ministry of the saints, setting the stage for prophetic leadership to assume newly-defined leadership roles. Another "next step" movement is emerging at the growing edges of the Body as Jesus moves the Church forward toward the Book of Acts.

Every prophetic leader must lead prophetic people in order to be successful. Elijah and John the Baptist both learned this difficult lesson early in their ministries. Because they had too few prophetic followers, their ministries appeared unsuccessful and they erroneously assumed personal failure. As with all prophetic leaders, their success was measured in the success of those they prophetically influenced. But prophecy is about fulfillment, and these prophetic leaders both fulfilled their assignments and released something that operated in an even bigger way than their own ministries!

The new leaders will do more than represent prophetic leadership; they will transform a prophetic people prepared to follow prophetic leaders. What begins with a remnant will sweep across the earth and help gather the greatest harvest of history!

Don't Limit God

No matter what program, personality, principle, or agenda drives churches, human motivations are too small to fulfill God's purposes! The problem with the conventional church is that it is too small! What is coming next will be marked by massive mini-movements that will move mega-church into even larger venues, but will also build mini-movements from what we have erroneously labeled "para-church" ministries. In truth, much of the conventional church is actually para-Church.[2]

When church attendance increases, men glory in their successes and feel like kings in their pulpits. If the church has bigger buildings and accumulates greater numbers of believers, men glory in their successes and point to their programs, personalities, principles, and purposes as sources and resources of spiritual success.

Idolatry says, "Look at this vision, this doctrine, this person, this purpose. This will get Father what He wants." It is just another substitute for the power of the Cross and the presence of Holy Spirit when it demands to be the source and resource of Kingdom building. Especially when it has the "if onlys" attached to it—"if only everyone would attend here, believe and do this, fulfill this vision, we would win the world in no time."

Don't limit God to that—beware of any idolatry! Church idolatry. Doctrinal idolatry. Personality idolatry. Vision idolatry. Idolatry substitutes something for Jesus and the church can be as guilty of idolatry as a Buddhist or sorcerer when it chooses another source and resource by which to fulfill her destiny.

Sometimes conventional church leaders want people because they need them to reach their goals, pay bills, prove worth, or establish the rightness of their teachings and strategies. People feel used, used up, and misused when "church" is more interested in investing them in fulfilling human objectives rather than in Father's purposes.

Leaders say with their actions and attitudes, "God will bring revival through us because we have the program." This is an example of *program*-centric leadership. Or, "Because our doctrine is right, God will reach our city through us." This is *principle*-centric leadership. "God is blessing and prospering this House because I am your leader," is *personality*-centric leadership. And, "Because we are focused on the purpose, we will succeed" is *purpose*-centric leadership.

No matter how wonderful the person, how right the principles, how efficient the program, or how worthy the purpose, the only Person must be Jesus, the only principles must be His opinions, the only program must be His agenda, and the only purpose must be Father's. A fresh revelation of Jesus, His mission strategy, His fulfilling truth, and His Father's purpose must be given to prophetic people and leaders in their generation. This fresh revelation resets and recalibrates the whole Body to what Jesus is doing here and now.

We can hardly expect to fulfill Father's purpose without His help. In fact, Jesus assures us we can do nothing to get Father what He wants without Him. Jesus says He is the True Vine and we are the branches: "You can do nothing apart from Me." (See John 15:5.) Jesus says, "You need to be presence-driven."

This is the trap of program, personality, principle, and purpose. If satan cannot keep you from the Cross altogether, he will work to get you to substitute human virtue for the power of the Cross. The Gospel has power because of the Cross, and any substitute diminishes ministry with humanly designed vision, humanly designated measurement, and humanly defined success. Substitutes frustrate the power of the Cross.

The Vision of the Mechanical Lamb

As the vision unfolded, I was in the balcony of a large, modern church building, one of those fan-shaped churches that seats two or three thousand people. The lighting, seating, flooring, and interior decorating were excellent. I liked the design. It was filling up with people as I looked on, as if the time of the church service was approaching. It looked as if the place was going to be packed full!

I saw that the ceiling had a track much like a miniature train track mounted above the people in such a way that something moving on the track would traverse the entire sanctuary.

On the track above the people, a motorized, artificial lamb moved back and forth from one wall to the other, silent and unobserved. Back and forth, back and forth.

Puzzled, I began to scrutinize this strange mechanical lamb. The mechanism that moved the lamb's legs, head, and body was hidden beneath real lamb's wool and the feet and nose were painted shiny black. It looked very real, but the eyes were dead.

Then, I noticed something very strange: the mechanical lamb was sprinkling the people with artificial blood! An inner reservoir was filled with this artificial substance and a tiny pump was pressurizing the spray so a very fine mist of fake blood was being sprinkled all over the congregation. No one below seemed to notice and everyone seemed happy. I was struck with the comfort and satisfaction the people felt with their church's ministry. A mechanical lamb with artificial blood sprinkling a modern church setting seemed absolutely normal to them!

The Substitution of the Artificial

The Bible speaks of sprinkling blood as a sign of the redemptive work for cleansing and preparation to come into God's presence. The artificial lamb and blood substituted for the real thing seemed absurd and grotesque. The prophetic vision continued...

As I watched and some efforts at worship began on the platform, something changed with the mechanical lamb. It was a gradual change, and no one noticed at first, but I could sense the lamb was moving more rapidly.

The Spirit and Power of Elijah

Greater expectations had been placed upon the mechanical lamb and as it moved faster, the humming noise that I had noticed steadily increased.

The people were really not so happy after all! Demands were being laid upon the mechanics of human ministry, placing a greater strain on the mechanical lamb.

As I looked on, the lamb's movements became increasingly erratic, even frantic, as it tried to keep up with a demand that it was not designed to meet. The installed systems were overloading. The tiny motors that moved the legs and head were whirling. Strained parts were overheating. The sprinkling changed from spray to droplets. Some of the drops were hitting people below.

I noticed then that the people were looking up with concern and consternation. They were clearly disappointed, disapproving, and disgusted. Some began to gather their belongings and leave.

The lamb seemed to respond with alarm and even greater urgency. Soon the lamb was running so fast that it banged into the walls and its wool began to come off. The motors that moved the lamb's legs and head were smoking, and a terrible screeching noise could be heard. Spraying blood gushed out of broken plumbing, and people were leaving in larger groups to avoid the spray.

As I watched, the lamb's whole system fell apart. Wool flew and blood sprayed. Oil and smoke came from the motors. The lamb moved with terrible jerking motions, grotesque and terrifying. The lamb was coming apart before my eyes!

Immediately, the vision changed...

The Champion Arrives to Claim His Church

The back of the platform opened into another vision.

The distant horizon was filled with a marching army. In the center, the Champion was riding a white horse. At first I could not distinguish His features.

Hovering over the Champion, a great white dove spread his wings wide, moving with the figure on the white horse. In the vision, the whole horizon was moving forward, and as I entered this part of the vision, the horizon began to move quickly toward the back of the church's platform.

Then, the Champion waved His hand, and signaled the white dove. It flew into the sanctuary with amazing speed. Swoosh! The dove hovered over the congregation like a jetliner and His great white wings stirred the air until every person was affected by the shaking and stirring.

Now I could see the Champion! It was Jesus, the Lamb of God wounded and sacrificed, but risen and full of eternal life! He rushed forward, jumped from the horse with ten thousand angels at either side, and stepped through the spiritual veil right into the sanctuary itself!

He was at once both beautiful and terrible, stepping onto the platform, center stage. And it was apparent He had come to claim it all for Himself! His eyes were flames of fire as He set His feet and turned His head from side to side as if to challenge everything and everyone in the house. He was staking a claim on His church!

Above us, the artificial lamb hung broken, silent, and forgotten. Jesus had come to His Church to claim it as His own.

Artificial Alternatives

Unfortunately when revival begins, leaders will examine the move of God from their own points of view. Because they have invested so much in their respective programs, personalities, principles, and purposes, they will have a much more difficult time accepting disruptive revival.

They ask this question, "Will this move of God help my program? Will this show everyone that I am the one who is right? Will I be one of the leaders? Will this move of God help me fulfill my purpose?"

Human programs are not an improvement on God's program, and He has never given up responsibility for setting the Church's agenda. Each new popular program may have the potential of restoring some aspect of God's program lost to the Church, but that aspect must be added to the mission Jesus gave the Church. Jesus started His own ministry and passed it on to the Church. Every programmed ministry model must fulfill Jesus' ministry. It must release life and transformation.

Perhaps programmed ministry vision can be a great tool to briefly refocus the energies of the Church on Jesus' ministry. It can also become a major distraction. I have seen great small group models destroy churches while releasing explosive growth in others. The ones that explode with life are built upon the foundations of intercession and transformational leadership.

However, no presently existing program will fit the next season because some basic definitions are being changed to reflect the mind of God. The vision-driven ministries that are successfully building the Body are all prophetic precursors moving the Church nearer to fullness. They are not fullness in themselves.

Principle-centric leaders are not preparing the Lord a people. Certainly the Church operates on God's principles, but nothing should be more obvious to the intellectually honest soul than the reality that no one branch, flavor, or movement of the Church has a corner on God's principles. God isn't interested in pushing any one aspect of revelation or operation to prove that aspect right.

Much of the Church's division is based on doctrinal idolatry, pride, and the worship of a chosen set of distinctives. The chosen distinctives define the division: "We exist separately from the rest of the Body, distinct from them, because we are the ones who emphasize these principles." In reality, the distinctives were chosen for emphasis, to correct a long-forgotten error, or to defend something that needs no defense.

Most principle-centric churches are carrying a former season's emphasis into the next season and trying to define the next season with it. This turns the former season's breakthrough into a brazen serpent idol. (Read the full story in Numbers 21:4-9 and Second Kings 18:4.)

The personality-centric church is a deformation of the goal of making the personality of Jesus central to His Body. Efforts to "return the integrity of leadership to the Body" or to "finally get people to do it the way they should" or to "honor the wonderful work this person has done in the church" may substitute honoring human personality for glorifying Jesus.

Only God has the responsibility to determine the measure of a man's ministry, and the honor due any leader is the honor due every leader. To honor the position Jesus has given is greater than honoring the personality fulfilling that position. Personality-centric ministries actually cause disrespect for leadership in general, leaving the impression that only certain leaders measured by some human rule of success are worthy of respect.

Personality-centric churches wait for God's great moment of personal promotion, as if God is a heavenly professional talent agent. God is not going to be your promotional agent. Personality-centric ministry is over! Jesus is coming to claim His church, to personally take over.

Purpose-driven is a new buzz word in the Church, and a good one! The concept is wholesome, powerful, appropriate, and biblical—as long as the purpose is Father's, not man's. We have suffered from purpose-driven church for centuries when the purpose driving the Body was human. In fact, the worst atrocities in history have often been done in the name of God, driven by human purpose.

Unfortunately, some leaders in the church are using the purpose-driven concept to reinforce their worn-out human purposes. They will either reject the move of God completely or seek to use the next move of God for their own purposes. Without prophetic preparation, we will miss the prophetic purposes of the next season, and continue to invest billions of dollars and millions of destinies fulfilling human purposes.

ENDNOTE

1. George Barna, *The State of the Church*, 2002.

2. A **para-church** ministry usually stands outside of the organization of recognized religious structures, autonomous with much greater receptivity to change than allowable within organizational hierarchies. Para-church represents the prophetic leadership of a spiritual entrepreneur or movement passionate to achieve specific assignments.

While often identified as a phenomenon of the awakenings, it presents revolutionary revival movements and models of Church history where prophetic leaders ignited something outside "what is" in order to prepare God's people for "what is coming next" in their generations. Usually identified para-church organizations would be tract societies, educational institutions, missionary groups, and cultural reform movements. I would see the para-church as the source leadership for revolutionary revival, great awakening, reformation, and evangelism in every season Father gives the Church Body. When the church moves away from its true priorities, Jesus redefines "church" outside the institutions and reestablishes foundational leadership so He can achieve what He wants with His Body.

6

Presence-Driven Leaders

Presence-Driven Leadership

Prophetic leaders are moving away from the substitutes and receiving transformation! Yes! Revival has a purpose only God knows completely, a purpose far above any human purpose, principle, person, or program. The Church is a purpose-driven Body!

God has purposes that the Church is established, called, anointed, and sent to fulfill. But the purpose that drives the Body of Christ can only be fulfilled with leaders driven by God's presence.

Sadly, the Church with its human purposes, heavy with more resources than ever, is failing miserably to fulfill God's purposes.

Leaders, the spirit and power of Elijah will not prepare a people for your purposes! It is not available to your culture and generation for any vision or purpose of man, any human institution or denomination. God is not trying to destroy these things men have created. He simply ignores them.

The move of God will change everything. It will make these human responses much less important and significant. They may blow away in His wind, burn up in His fire, or simply fade away in His glory.

The traps of human substitution close tightly. Because none of these things is evil of itself, the traps appear harmless and sometimes even holy. The traps are set with things worthy, noble, awesome, and "Christian." The traps fit comfortably around our necks because the sound, flavor, smell, and appearance are consistent with our pretty experiences. (We sometimes call them "yokes.") They feel all the more vital to us because we think we control them.

God is about to destroy those traps. God is about to expand our understanding! Will you receive it? Or, will you rebuild the traps God destroys?

Receive prophetic insight! Receive a refining fire! Receive prophetic leadership! Will you look for it? Seek it? God is sending what you need to get ready for His visitation and a last-days harvest like none ever seen in history! The spirit and power of Elijah is preparing a people for the Lord! Jesus is planning to arrive and take over His Church and be the only Head! He will come and be the only source and resource. He will speak, and every other voice will speak as His! Will you receive it?

The phrase "go ahead of Him" tells us God is sending a forerunner, someone to "get there first" and "get things ready." God is preparing His people by sending them very special prophetic voices housed in very special prophetic people.

Hey! He's a Preacher!

I have always known I was a preacher. In previous decades, doctors were known to lift a newborn up by the ankles and slap the child to make him cry and breathe deeply, expanding his lungs. This introduced him to his new world, a world in which he would need to breathe on this own.

The scene: "Hey! Congratulations, it's a boy!" Wham! While Mother joyfully weeps and Dad pridefully beams, baby gets a rude reception from his first "outside" encounter with humanity. Baby is welcomed into the world with a stiff rap to the rear!

When I was born, I was so ugly the doctor couldn't figure out where to slap me. Finally, after looking over the landscape for a ready place to land a blow, he just closed his eyes and whacked me.

I was incensed! I screamed loudly. My face turned purple and I promptly drenched the front of his sterile suit. My lungs were operating just fine. The doctor heard my enormous mouth open widely and scream for the first time and the doctor said, "A preacher!"

I've always known that was my destiny. John the Baptist always knew his as well.

Alive for a Purpose

John is indeed very special. Jesus says so! You are just as special as John the Baptist. You are alive right now because God wanted you alive, wanted you to be born, and wanted your destiny to be fulfilled here and now.

The angel released a creative word into the earth that would bring about the conception of John; it was a word from the very heart of God. This announcement set in motion a timetable, a schedule of events long-anticipated and forever understood to have been the very center of history.

Events that appear unimportant can often initiate shifts in history that eternally alter entire nations. Without ears to hear and eyes to see, such prophetic events may occur right in front of us without our recognizing their significance.

God weighs this human event heavy with potential. Elizabeth feels she is carrying a baby, but really she is carrying much, much more! John's first cry sounds a call to Heaven and earth and brings both worlds to account. A baby's cry releases Israel's greatest call, a voice crying in the wild places to a people poised above the chasm, about to step off into the precipice of a powerful disaster.

God was about to visit His creation, fulfilling a divine expectation—God had waited centuries to see His will and purpose for Israel fulfilled in Messiah—and His visitation would bring the highest glory of God into the earth and the greatest judgment of human failure to a chosen people.

John the Baptist is a pivotal person upon whose life and ministry Israel's destiny swivels and turns, first toward life and hope, then toward ruin and despair. God chose unlikely people to birth an unlikely son for an unlikely ministry in an unlikely time. God chose to do things in a way that only He could receive glory for the outcome.

God is working like this in your life. You are a pivotal person! What He is doing no one else can do. God will do something in you only God can do, and it is something you can do nothing to earn, appropriate, or demand. All you can do is surrender and receive!

We tend to separate what God is doing in the earth from what we are doing for God in the earth. Without prophetic leadership in our own lives and in the Church, we tend to do our own thing and let God do His.

But He Seems so Odd

Don't allow yourself to miss God by prejudging or rejecting His unusual representatives because their style of ministry is unusual or their anointings are different. This is exactly what you should expect from the special messengers God sends. Consider that they may not be the unusual ones. Because God sent them, they are "normal" to Him. Perhaps we are the ones who seem aberrant to God because He is already acting upon the basis of the next season!

God sends passionate leaders to people He intends to visit in order to shake those people, change them, and prepare them for something new. He wants His people to be passionate as well. Before God visits any people, they are never really ready for His presence and power. He is always far ahead of present human progress.

Preparatory leaders bring unusual ministry to prepare people for unusual visitation. Prophetic leaders appear unusual because they operate in the spirit and power of the One they are preparing people to receive, not their own or some human dynamic.

Jesus is unusual. Jesus has unusual leadership. Jesus operates in unusual authority and power. So the prophetic leaders He sends to prepare His people seem unusual as well.

We can see from the phrase "he will go ahead of Him" that someone else is coming; someone is coming for a visit! The objective of the forerunner is preparation, to introduce the spirit and power of the coming Visitor. Something of the heart and mind of the One who is coming must be instilled into the situation in order for the people to be ready to receive and process the Coming One's arrival.

God is sending the Church prophetic leaders because Jesus is a prophetic leader. We can be certain He is looking for prophetic people because the voice of the Lord will be more easily heard. God's revelations will be more frequently received, and God's prophets will be more readily received—flaws and all. Prophetic people follow prophetic leadership because they sense it will lead them to the heart of God.

The Church will be embarrassed during this season if she is not filled with prophetic people. God is coming for a visit, and we would not wish history to reveal us ill-prepared; or worse, reveal that we rejected His visitation because we failed to recognize Him at all.

THE DAY OF PROPHETIC LEADERS

As mentioned previously, when I speak of the spirit and power of Elijah, I am not referring to prophecy gift operations, nor am I speaking only of prophets in a simpler, localized sense. I am describing prophetic leaders sent by God as the prophetic element of the fivefold ministry, a foundational leadership function of the Body.

I am making a clear distinction because the fuller restoration and function of all five aspects of Jesus' ministry has opened the door for a fuller expression of each of them. Prophetic leadership will be more than it has been since Pentecost.

Prophetic leaders include all the functions and offices of the fivefold expression of Jesus and are all about preparing prophetic people. Jesus is lifting the Body of Christ into a position of fulfilling God's purposes, not just understanding or recognizing them. The distinction means we are well past the "this prophetic stuff is real!" stage and into the "God has revealed a strategy for this culture and we are going to implement it" stage.

Prophetic leaders are first leaders. They work together to fulfill and execute God's decisions. All God's people can be prophetic people and must be prepared to live and minister prophetically—all are leaders at some level, but not all are leaders at the same level. They flow into a mighty river of prophetic implementation, and these streams are fed by other prophetic leaders.

Today's Prophetic Operations

The modern Church is leery of prophecy because hell has made them inordinately sensitive to errant prophecy. However, false, inept, and inexperienced teachers, evangels, pastors, and apostles do not make the Church leery of all teachers, evangels, pastors, and apostles. Therefore, false, less-than-accurate, and inexperienced prophets should not make the Church leery of *all* prophets.

Remember the words of Paul concerning prophetic ministry: "Do not extinguish the Spirit. Do not discount prophecies. Test all of them. Seize hold of the good; push away every evil viewpoint" (1 Thess. 5:21).

The Word of God makes it clear that false prophecy is as prevalent as false teaching, and disagreements and differences in points of view will always be available within the Church. Pushing away all prophecy is a direct contradiction of the Word of God! Of course, seizing onto and seeking after every prophetic word is just as ridiculous and unscriptural.

Test all prophecies. Test all prophetic leadership. Be mature sons and daughters. Do not attach yourselves to people who speak what you wish to hear flavored with some form of prophetic speech, prophesying great things so you will rejoice in those who give the words.

The purpose of prophecy is either to confirm or reveal God's decisions and purposes to His people so they will be ready to respond to what He is doing in their culture in their generation. Prophecy is always about God's will, not ours. Prophecy is about purposes God has created and called each of us to fulfill. Prophecy is about redemptive purposes for every culture under Heaven as God created and designed each culture to produce special, significant aspects of His Kingdom culture in the earth. Prophetic leadership is foundational leadership designed to release fulfillment of God's decisions and purposes on earth.

Responding to Confrontation

John the Baptist mistook the absence of a prophetic people for personal failure. Jesus promptly responded to John's concerns about his own ministry and the potential for His ultimate success. Jesus turned to the crowd following Him and further clarified the spirit and power of Elijah released ahead of His ministry.

In Matthew 11:9-15, Jesus asks:

What did you go out to see? A prophet? Yes, I say to you, and more than a prophet! For of him it is written, "See! I send my messenger before your presence to prepare your path in front of you." I tell you truly, among those woman-born none has arisen greater than John the Baptist. However, the least in the Kingdom of Heaven is greater than he. During the days of John the Baptist until now, people pressed toward the Kingdom of Heaven and fought to take it by force. For all the prophets and the law prophesied until John. And if you are willing to accept it, this is Elijah, which was to come. He that has ears to hear let him hear.

Anyone may reject the move of God, and you will be shocked observing which people reject or receive what God is doing. Some of God's best people have "too much to lose" to alter their ministries and lives to fit God's here and now priorities.

Confrontation precedes the arrival of God's day, a precursor of preparation. Confrontation turns some people toward God and others away from Him. Confrontation sets a new spiritual base line and temporarily makes all of us uncomfortable, but it is absolutely necessary to get people ready to respond to the Lord.

Why do people reject the sent messengers of God? Why did Jesus' generation kill Him as their forefathers had killed prophets before Him? Obvious recompenses were passed to Jesus' generation from centuries of rebellion against God's purpose. While all the prophets and the law prophesied for the Kingdom of Heaven, people sought to enter it by human force and power instead of obedience to prophetic leadership.

Until John arrived to prepare people for the Lord's coming, no heavenly kingdom was possible because no heavenly king was available to rule it. Although Israel won some marginal victories in the years preceding John's appearance, people weren't prepared for the Lord. A remnant in each generation preserved and reserved God's purpose, but the fulfillment was still a deferred hope.

Jesus clarifies and identifies John's ministry: "If you are willing to receive it, to accept his ministry, he is Elijah prophesied to arrive before Me."

I have been in church all my life. My grandfather was a pastor. My father is a pastor. My brother and I are pastors. I have been in ministry since I was 15. I know "church." Church is all about conformity, comfort, and convention. It is not what Jesus did and is inconsistent with His nature and disposition, but the religious cycle begins subtly, silently, and softly.

Breaking the Cycle

The cycle consists of false expectations and human effort. Only confrontation breaks the cycle, but the church cycle defines leadership as protection from the required confrontation. Leaders who break the cycle also shatter the leadership paradigm of "church."

In the conventional church, leaders are trained to avoid confrontation because of the political nature of the internal relationships within the church organization. Confrontation is not politically productive—compromise is.

However, God is God, and God is confrontational. God is not moved by compromise, but is eternally committed to covenant. Covenant and confrontation pack up and travel in the same luggage. Covenant demands confrontation; organizational politics loathe it.

Take careful note of the phrase "if you are willing to accept it." While revival is a sovereign move of God, it is not inevitable on a large scale. God will revive the willing, and often the willing represents a remnant. God moves on with the willing and continues to reach out to the waiting. No guarantees of widespread awakening arrived with Elijah or John, but I believe Jesus has something for us in this generation that will blow the Church wide open! (In a good way, of course.)

It will be difficult to break out of the cycle—no, it will be impossible for us to break out of the cycle. Only armed with the power of the Cross can we repent and acquire a will strong enough to surrender.

I recall one of the first prophecies we ever received. A group of three seasoned prophets were speaking to Ruthanne and me about ministry. The first prophet said he saw a large, dark whirlpool and I was standing on the side of it. "You are stepping into something new in your ministry, and this whirlpool will suck you in if you allow it. You are going to be living right on the edge. Don't take one step toward that whirlpool."

I knew immediately what the dark whirlpool was. I had been living in it for most of my life. I was really surprised that this whirlpool operated in churches that were Spirit-filled.

A religious spirit will provide any substitute, any distraction to the ministry of Jesus. You can do all the good stuff you want and call it "ministry," and the enemy will be content. "Hey, knock yourself out!" he says. But immediately when you get into intercession, the ministry of Jesus, fulfilling God's purpose, and executing God's decisions, that dark whirlpool will work to suck you in.

I always stop myself and ask, "Is this all it takes to get me off track? Is this all it takes to shut down my intercession? Is this all it takes to distract me from passionate worship?"

Receiving the Elijah ministry and walking in it will require that you stay out of the religious, administrative whirlpool. For most pastors this means a complete overhaul of everyday living, but it is a required overhaul.

The ministry of John was a restoration ministry, but restoration comes only to those who accept it. Personal (and national) restoration comes only to those who accept it.

7

Elijah Prayer and Worship

PREPARATION IN PRAYER

Prophetic leaders are intercessors—they pray to God on behalf of others—and their intercession may be unlike any we have seen. Preparing people for the Lord introduces them to Father's heart through prayer.

The most powerful way to prepare a prophetic people with prophetic leadership is intercession. Nothing creates prophetic energy, capacity, and maturity like intercession! Everything flows into and out of intercession, and prophetic intercession prepares a prophetic people. Here is the only successful strategy leaders have to lead a prophetic people—pray with them as a prophetic leader.

Engaging people in the Spirit is the most intimate spiritual experience a leader can have. It is the best opportunity for shared spiritual experiences. The true sense of communing fellowship that the Scriptures insist is normal for Body members is realized when people are sharing spiritual experiences, when strong, loving leadership actively guides these experiences.

Intercession should be led by prophetic leaders. Most are. Internationally known prophetic leaders and local, directly involved, prophetic leaders give them insight and confirming revelation for what they are hearing and praying. They are not praying in a vacuum even though they belong to God in a special way and have a special calling of personal, intimate interaction with Him. They move to a higher place of effectiveness in seasons of revolutionary revival with prophetic leadership. Tens of thousands of intercessors are moving into spiritual unity for Father's purposes in the earth right now as prophetic leaders declare what God wants for cities and nations.

By this I mean that intercessors should step into a new place of intercession in seasons of revolutionary revival as prophetic leaders engage them more specifically in the assignments of their generations. They have been individually led by the Spirit, prophetically engaged in contending for what Father wants, but prophetic leadership allows them to connect their intercession with the remnant and create movements that impact cities and nations!

While every intercessor is not a prophet or prophetic leader, every leader actually functioning prophetically is an intercessor. True intercession touches Father's heart so the intercessor experiences His burning passion for His purposes. That is why a new intercession is coming to the Church, intercession at a new level without the silliness of previous caricatures of spirituality.

Training people in the United States and worldwide for ministry and leadership is one of the highest aspects of the ministry that Ruthanne and I have. In FreedomHouse and Ministry Matrix, we always baseline the preparation and implementation of ministry on times of intense, shared, and leader-guided intercession. If leaders can't faithfully and successfully pray with you, you probably don't want them ministering with you.

Want to know people? Get into the spirit with them. Want to really measure their spiritual capacities? Get into the spirit with them. Want to know their passion more than their potential? Get into the spirit with them.

When people have more to say about ministry and greater plans and strategies of ministry than their intercession for that ministry, you may rest assured they will inject more flesh than spirit into fulfilling ministry. Prophetic people are absolutely necessary to prophetic leadership, and prophetic people are best prepared in intercession led by prophetic leaders.

With Jesus in the School of Prayer

When I began to speak with a language I had never learned, to pray in languages of the spirit, I immediately became an intercessor. For me, the change was intense, immediate, profound, and long-lasting.

Having heard missionaries sing songs in the language of their nations of ministry, the battle to release this gift was a frightening thing for me. I just knew God was going to give me one of those strange, guttural languages with really hard consonant sounds. I just knew I would sound like a back-firing lawnmower every time I prayed, so I hesitated. It was simply a matter of deeply-seated pride!

One day as I drove my van home from a meeting, I opened my mouth and began to pray in a spiritual language...I prayed for eight hours...every day...for one year. I just couldn't stop praying!

During all of my previous ministry experiences, prayer had been the least of my activities. I knew better, but I simply did not pray very much. I could voice courtesy prayers at the hospital, over a meal, at a banquet or special occasion, and, of course, I spoke appropriate prayers in church, but I had no communion with God and no prayer life that supported my ministry. None.

Now, I found myself suddenly thrust into an intensive intercession school with Jesus. It was great!

I am an intercessor, and I would be happy praying full time. It is the work of ministry. Everything in ministry flows out of it and answers to it. Without it, ministry becomes mere human effort flowered with plastic blossoms, stuffed with religious fluff. Without intercession, ministry becomes a deadly sham.

I have helped train hundreds of intercessors, provided prophetic leadership for intercessors, traveled with intercessory prayer teams into other nations, cities, and regions, and been on assignments with God for intercession and spiritual warfare in the nations; and I tell you—I love the wonderful world of intercession!

Our ministry includes aspects of transformation, deliverance and inner healing, and leadership development. I have discovered in fulfilling these ministries that intercession is everyone's job. Every leader must first be an intercessor before he or she becomes a leader. In our school of ministry, every student learns to intercede before they learn to "do ministry."

God is releasing a new wave of intercession in the earth, equipping intercessors to partner with the spirit and power of Elijah that is preparing God's people for the great revival and harvest that is coming. No matter where you are now in intercession, it is time to step up to a new level. It is time to step into a new place. It is time to pray with greater authority, to pray bigger prayers, to partner with apostolic and prophetic leaders and to pray for nations.

The mantle of Elijah's intercession is available, and the prayer of a righteous person makes tremendous spiritual might available! To become more of a prophetic leader and prepare a prophetic people, you need to plan for strategic, prophetic intercession with your people.

James says the spiritual power of Elijah's ministry was evidenced in his prayer life. The spirit and power of Elijah releases a mantle for intercession that changes the heavens and transforms the earth. We have very specific examples of this relationship of intercession in the Old Testament; but in James we have a direct reference to prayer in which Elijah's mantle is a featured aspect of New Testament authority and power. (See James 5:17-18.)

Leaders, stop turning intercession over to someone else! Stop assigning intercession leadership to someone "who is not busy doing the work of ministry." Intercession is the ministry! Intercession, and its leadership, is not restricted to "women's work."

Leaders, if you are not spending scheduled, consistent times of intense intercession with your people, times you personally lead, you are not leading prophetically or preparing a prophetic people. No matter how many prophetic activities you think you are releasing, you are not leading prophetically or creating a prophetic people unless you are personally leading them in intercession.

Elijah's unique relationship with God spoke to the very foundation of his ministry—a restoration, intercessing prophet. Elijah not only personally prayed but led a nation back to their place of prayer. He healed the broken altar of their communion and covenant with God.

PREPARATION IN WORSHIP

The spirit and power of Elijah are evidenced in the worship he restored to Israel, rebuilding the altar of the Lord that was broken down, showing the foolish vanity of Baal worship—frenzied, slash-with-knives desperation disco.

And Elijah gathered all the people at Mount Carmel: "Come over here where I am." They all came near Elijah, and he repaired the broken-down altar of Jehovah (1 Kings 18:30).

The Hebrew word translated "repaired" is *rapha* which means "healing." Elijah healed the broken altar of worship wounded by covenant betrayal. The wounded worship was restored by a prophetic leader.

During a prophetic time in Brazil, God revealed this spiritual condition—wounded worship—and helped us heal a congregation. I don't know all that wounded the worship of this church, but I know God revealed a generational division and a betrayal of leadership as the cause of the wound. I heard the Lord say, "The worship of this house is wounded; the leaders and the people are wounded. Division and betrayal have opened them to bruising and their worship processes their 'woundedness.' Tonight I would heal them."

Bringing up a young man and an elderly gentleman from the front row, I stood them face to face and prophesied to the wounded worship. Facing the young man I declared: "One generation shall praise your works to another, and shall declare your mighty deeds." (See Psalm 145:4.)

"Now, young man," I declared, moving to stand with the younger man, facing the elderly gentleman, "this generation praises the works of God to you and declares that our God does mighty things! We declare that we accept and love your passionate worship, different but beautiful before Heaven. We release you to sing your songs, dance your dance, and worship your worship."

Pointing to the gray-haired gentleman, I said, "We declare that God who was faithful to this generation will be faithful to yours. There is no division."

God healed the worship of that house that night! I see God reaching into the Church all over the world to heal the worship where altars have been wounded by broken covenants!

At Carmel, Elijah says, "The God who responds to prayer and worship with fire will be the true God." The people said, "This is good." (See 1 Kings 18:38-39.)

In the Name of the Lord

The prophet rebuilt or repaired the wounded altar: "Elijah built an altar in the Name of the Lord." (See 1 Kings 18:32.) How does Elijah build an altar "in the name of the Lord," in the authority of the Lord? How does anyone build an altar that establishes God's authority?

The Spirit and Power of Elijah

How can we build altars in the name of the Lord here and now?

It is certain that millions of people say, "We worship Jesus. We are Christians." Yet, many of our altars of worship are not built in the name of the Lord. God is confronting us in the spirit and power of Elijah as He did in Jesus' generation through John the Baptist. They said, "We worship Jehovah as Moses instructed us. We are Abraham's children." Yet, their altars were not built in the name of the Lord.

God is confronting people who worship on altars of their own design and creation, who are bringing God worship that they want Him to have instead of worship that He has created.

Elijah built an altar "in the name of the Lord" to establish the Lordship of Jehovah, to make Him King of that place and time. The rebuilding was more than a symbol, ceremony, or sacrament. Elijah was building an altar that made Jehovah King, and all the people were party to this encounter of power and allegiance.

Such worship is the kind of worship designed by God Himself and created to establish His presence and power in a nation, to make God Lord of a people. Every altar built in the authority of the Lord gives Him dominion of the place and time of that sacrifice.

You have authority and power! You can rebuild broken, wounded altars—in the spirit and power of Elijah.

In Brazil, for example, the worship we are experiencing is powerful because we are building altars of worship that make Jesus Lord of the place and time. We are worshiping in such a way that Jesus is given dominion, and

He ascends to His proper place of kingly reign in our worship. It is worship that pushes back the power of hell, because it displaces the false claims made on Brazil. Brazil belongs to Jesus Christ! Prophetic worship restores dominion by establishing His Lordship.

In Brazil, the passion of worship—in song, with instruments and dance, with abandoned expressions of total devotion—is building altars in the name of Jesus that leaves no room for false worship, for witchcraft, for dead religion, or for spiritual substitutes.

It is worship that flows from the very heart of the Father; His passionate love for Jesus and Brazil flows through us and is expressed in living sacrifices. We are releasing ourselves, our bodies, our voices, and our passionate love to Him.

Such worship builds an altar in the name of the Lord and establishes the rule of God in the place and time. Such worship is created by God and released by Holy Spirit through healed and holy hearts.

This is the spirit and power of Elijah! It is worship that makes Jesus Lord. God is calling us to this kind of worship, and we must move on from where we are to where God is. It is the worship of the next season expressed in a remnant, gaining momentum, overtaking the status quo; and we are in final rehearsal. The spirit and power of Elijah provides prophetic leadership to heal our worship altars and establish God's Kingdom!

God Creates Worship

Only God can create Kingdom worship. Everywhere worship is described or enjoined in Scripture, God designs and creates the worship; and people respond to His designs and commands. They fulfill and release what God creates. God never gives men the responsibility to decide how and when Kingdom worship should occur. Men release God's created worship, and He responds to the worship He has designed and created.

This is the difference between what prevails in church and what the spirit and power of Elijah restores and releases. The conventional church falls into the trap of offering God worship created by men, prescribed by men, and released in human will. This worship may be beautiful in artistic terms, majestic in appearance, and poetic in its descriptions and expressions of praise and thanksgiving, but it is created by men. It is not Kingdom worship.

It is not evil, but it lacks spirit and power. It is not satanic, but it is not redemptive. It mentions God and Jesus, but it does not release or establish His Lordship; it mixes the sentiments of men, the desires and designs of men with forms of religious expression. It cannot release the passion of God because it begins and ends with the will of man. When we release worship created by God, God is released.

When Jesus rode into Jerusalem on a colt, a song broke out, a traditional song to be sure, but a traditional song that became something else. The worship that operated in this moment established Jesus' Lordship and released power in prophetic praise. Their song became a prophetic release when Father created worship in the mouths of children. The song had been sung as part of the ritual of choosing the lambs for Passover, but the children began to sing with something beyond religious tradition. "Hosanna" became a prophetic cry. *Hosanna* means "save us!" The prayer request became a prophetic declaration by anointing and divine power.

It was not the miracles that broke out in the Temple that offended the religious leaders, it was the song of the children.

"Can't you make them stop singing? Can't you shut those kids up!" they demanded.

In answering those who objected to this prophetic song, Jesus quoted from the Psalms, "Out of the mouths of infants and nursing babies you have provided powerful praise" (Ps. 8:2). The Hebrew word translated *praise* sometimes means "power" and other times "praise." The song of the children released and established the power of God, and at that moment blind eyes were opened and lame people began to walk!

What We Want God to Have

The worship of Cain does not establish Kingdom Lordship on earth, and we, like Cain, may easily stumble into the snare of offering God what we want Him to have instead of what He created to release through us.

Abel worshiped as God had created and designed, and he was received. Cain brought God what he wanted God to have and was angry and arrogant when God did not receive his offering. God quickly pointed out to Cain that his sacrifice would be received if he brought an acceptable offering, when he responded to God's designed and created worship. But Cain was angry, and his aggression turned jealousy into murder. (See Genesis 4.)

The conventional church designs and creates worship, then brings the worship to God and says, "Now, Lord, we are doing this in your name, so bless what we have created for you." The conventional church gives God what the conventional church wants God to have.

Yet, God is not impressed with good people doing good things in good churches just because what they do is done in His name. This worship does not establish the authority of God. It establishes the authority of men, the authority of men who determine what God wants almost as if He has no voice or involvement in the worship at all.

How easily we are ensnared by pride and arrogance. How easily God gets us out of it when we surrender. Our yielding and brokenness, the very essence of Kingdom worship, breaks us through the sham. Father is searching the earth for those who worship Him in spiritual reality.

The spirit and power of Elijah restores and releases a new sound, a sound created by God in prophetic song and insight, a sound of passionate praise from anointed people lost in wonder and worship in the presence and power of Holy Spirit.

We are seeing this Kingdom worship in many nations. Our worship is releasing Holy Spirit, worship created by God and released into time in tune with Heaven—we are releasing the sound of Heaven into the earth!

Establish the Lordship of Jesus

Much of the prayer that flows from and through the conventional church springs from religious validations more than spiritual motivations. Men request divine blessing upon good activities of good people in good churches: "Bless these works of men now presented to God." They offer prayers that seek to establish the will of man, but the spirit and power of Elijah is a mantle of prayer that establishes the Lordship of Jesus.

Notice that Elijah first prayed to shut down the rain. For more than three years the power of Baal, the thunderstorm and rain god worshiped by Jezebel, was shown to be less powerful than the power of Jehovah. Baal was and is no god at all! Because the people worshiped Baal as the god who controlled the skies and weather, seeking to appease this god so he would provide rain, Jehovah instructed Elijah to pray and shut up the heavens.

It is important to notice that God told Elijah to pray this, that the prayer of Elijah was a prayer God gave him, a prayer God revealed to be His will, a prayer that would accomplish God's purpose. It was not prayer from Elijah's "bad hair day" anger or his personal disgust with Ahab, Jezebel, and Israel.

It is also important to notice that God did not shut up the heavens without good reason; God instructed Elijah to pray this prayer so God's authority and power would be established. God revealed His will to Elijah, and then Elijah released God's will into the earth through prayer. Elijah did not decide to bring a drought on Israel of his own volition or reveal his own power and authority.

Elijah prayed a prayer directed by God that established God's authority and power, to reveal that Baal was no god at all, and to bring the people to God's offer of transformation on Carmel. They could no longer continue to worship both Baal and Jehovah after the showdown on Carmel.

We have this mantle of prayer available here and now!

New Testament Prayer Power

James tells us Elijah's prayer is a prayer of power and authority, a prayer God wants His people to pray now—it is not for a special moment in history or only for one man with an unusual ministry. The spirit and power of Elijah operates to restore powerful prayer to the Body of Christ.

James says: "The prayer of one righteous person makes much prevailing spiritual strength available. Elijah was a man with passion like ours; and he prayed that it should not rain and it did not rain on earth three years and six months. Then he prayed again, and heaven gave rain and earth produced fruit." (See James 5:16-18.)

James speaks to us about authority and power in prayer and makes a special point of the spiritual might available in Elijah by prayer. He makes it very apparent that this anointing in prayer is available today.

God used Elijah when the prophet prayed what God told him, and one righteous person makes the same prevailing spiritual might available when he prays God's will today.

The word James uses for *power* means "spiritual might." It is used only of God or spiritual beings, a word used to speak of controlling weather, storms, and prevailing over spiritual darkness. It is not human strength and is different from the *dunamis* power of Pentecost. It is spiritual power in the heavenlies where God and angels live. This strength is released through the Elijah mantle of prayer to establish God's will, to cause His will to come to pass in earth as it is in Heaven.

God is raising up intercessors who pray His will, who pray what He reveals to them, who pray to establish God's Lordship. They are not praying to bless human programs and agendas. They are praying prayers that release God's strength, pushing back the claims of hell over people, homes, cities, and regions. They are making great spiritual strength available like the power Elijah released to shut up the heavens and open them again!

The spirit and power of Elijah included a mantle of prayer and worship that established who God is, that confronts witchcraft, idolatry, satanism, and false religion. It is praying God's will to pass! Those who stand in the way of God's will in the heavens or the earth will give way to this kind of intercession. Everyone who is righteous can pray God's will covered with Elijah's mantle of prayer! This is what Jesus taught us to pray.

Jesus Shows Us How to Pray (See Matthew 6:9-13.)

First, hallow and sanctify the name and authority of the Father.

"I hallow your name."

This is not a restatement of "Thou shalt not take the name of the Lord thy God in vain." It is a fulfillment of the law and prophets, an act of will, a choice to hallow God's name and authority with awe and worship.

An anointing rests heavily upon declarations and songs that affirm, "There is no God like the Lord" and

"The God of the Bible is the only God." We begin prayer with worship, declaring reverential awe before God, choosing Him, worshiping Him, and lifting His Name to a proper place of preeminence in the place and time of our prayer and declaration.

Such a declaration changes all spiritual conditions around us. It is our first step in intercession and prayer, in any worship and ministry.

Second, declare the arrival of God's Kingdom.

"Kingdom of God arrive!"

This declaration is spoken as a prophetic command: "Kingdom of God arrive!" We use the imperative voice, the voice that commands.

Much like the "Hosanna" declared by the crowds when Jesus arrived in the city of Jerusalem, the request becomes a declaration, releasing and establishing authority and power. "Hosanna" is a prayer which means "Save us!" and became a prophetic declaration to Jesus' generation.

Now, bring this voice and attitude to the prayer Jesus teaches us to pray: "Kingdom of God arrive!" Move from requesting to declaring. Make a positive, humble recognition that Jesus is King, and declare the spiritual reality of His Lordship where you are when you speak. Kingdom reality is being established "here and now" when we worship and praise with prophetical declaration.

Third, declare God's will is happening.

"Will of God happen!"

Jesus says we should declare God's ruling presence and power—when Jesus is Lord here and now the will of the King will be carried out. When God reigns, He gets what He wants.

The declaration reveals how God the King acts when He is King of a place and time and people. It says, "When the Kingdom of God arrives, He is King. When He is King, His will is done in the Kingdom. This is how God treats His people when He is King."

When Elijah prayed, Israel fell on their faces at the revelation of the true God and cried, "Jehovah, He is God! Jehovah, He is God!" They made a choice between Baal and Jehovah. They established the rule of Jehovah in their hearts and over their land. This is the mantle of prayer God is releasing with the spirit and power of Elijah.

The mantle is not about style or content. It is about the spirit and power that operates when restoration leaders prepare people for the Lord's visitation.

A New Intercession

Intercession is a very good word. It is a Bible word; and it is especially important because it is a term that gathers all the elements of prayer, worship, and authority that God has been restoring within the Church. We have been appropriately referring to the changes we have experienced and seen in a new level of prayer with word intercession. This new level has been operating in the Body of Christ for more than 20 years.

Some rather unfortunate things have happened in the name of intercession during this time of restoration. Some rather unfortunate things have also happened in the name of preaching, missionary work, marriage, church, offerings, and many other aspects of ministry. None of these unfortunate things should drive us to reject the validity of intercession.

It is time for a new army of intercessors, and a new level of intercession.

Some used to consider "intercessors" as the odd women of the church who gathered for prayer in the home of a strange woman. These days are over! Intercessors are not weird people—and they are not always women. While I have trained hundreds of people in intercession and most of those I have trained have been women, it is wrong to assume intercession is "women's work."

I am a man. I am an intercessor. While there are reasons why men have not entered into this fellowship of spiritual authority as they should have, the time has come for fundamental corrections in the area of intercession. It is time for the Elijah mantle of prayer to settle upon the shoulders of men *and* women.

The spirit and power of Elijah has nothing to do with gender. It is not more available to men or women. It is not available for prophetic leadership for men exclusive of women. It is a mantle that touches every aspect of intercession with prophetic flavor.

Every intercessor is not being promoted to prophetic leadership. Every worshiper is not stepping into a pulpit. However, the ministry God has released, for preparing His people, a new level of intercession and worship, and prophetic leaders must be leaders in intercession and worship.

The next level releases new intercessors prepared to intercede and worship with the prophetic leaders. All over the world God is raising up this new army of intercessors. I, for one, intend to help bring more people into the ranks and train them in this vital role, to partner with God and His purposes in the earth.

8

Our Time of Visitation

IF YOU RECEIVE IT

Jesus is saying, "If you accept it, the spirit and power of Elijah has arrived to restore all, and this restoration prepares a people for the day of my visitation."

Even the fact that Jesus Himself visited the generation of John the Baptist did not guarantee full restoration. The move of God arrived to restore, but the restoration prepared only the people who received its power. God preserved a purpose for His chosen people, used a preserved mantle to restore His purpose in the day of the Lord's visitation; but the anointing of the prophet priest, John the Baptist, was rejected. So was Jesus.

So, we conclude with certainty and a deepening sense of awe that rejecting the prophetic leadership sent in the spirit and power of Elijah sets us up to reject the move of God when it arrives. Unless we walk in the confrontation, the restoration, the transformation that prophetic leadership brings, we will not be ready for the revival. We will reject the move of God in our generation.

Israel's end was sealed by their rejection of John's spirit and power because without the preparation of that anointing, they could not be ready to embrace their Messiah, Jesus. Some may have "avoided" John's preparation ministry more than they rejected it. However, before we step back from the word "reject" we would be wise to consider that *neglect* is rejection when it comes to receiving what God is doing in our generation.

Jesus wept over Jerusalem, "If you knew—if not before at least today—the things released to provide your peace...but even now they have been hidden from your eyes! For days will come upon you when your enemies will raise up a rampart against you, will surround you, trap you on all sides, and destroy you and your children with you, and will not leave one stone upon another stone because you did not recognize the time of your visitation" (Luke 19:41-44).

The Time of *Your* Visitation

"You did not recognize the time of your visitation"— no generation or culture can long endure the epitaph of such prophetic failure! Father raised the level of prophetic ability and awareness in Israel during the Jesus generation so they could prepare for His visitation, but they hid their eyes and refused to become a prophetic people responding to the prophetic leadership He sent them.

I tell you, God is raising the level of prophetic ability and awareness during this generation to prepare for His visitation and secure a prophetic response in the next generation. He wants us ready to walk out the fullness of His visitation! A remnant is opening their eyes, and the greatest army of prophetic people history has ever seen is networking all over the world to respond to the spirit and power of Elijah in these last days.

God is releasing more than revelatory insight, the spirit of prophecy, prophetic gifts, and prophets. He is giving the Church prophetic leaders. Look for them now! We have had incredible prophetic voices in the past, fathers of the prophetic movement, but most of them were not leaders. They were valid prophets, and we bless them, but God is bringing a new generation of prophetic leaders. We will have the spirit of prophecy, prophetic gifts, and prophets who are not leaders, but we will also see prophetic leadership moving in the spirit and power of Elijah. These prophetic people release transformational leadership into cities, regions, and cultures of the earth.

Israel, in John's day, did not recognize and receive the spirit and power of Elijah to prepare the Lord a people, so God prepared a remnant to pick up what Israel had left unfulfilled. A Roman army moved across Israel, destroying the land on their way up to Jerusalem. They destroyed the city and finally broke down the Temple walls to reach the last hold-outs of Jewish opposition who barricaded themselves in the Temple to avoid the advancing army. After setting the temple on fire, Romans separated every stone to retrieve the cherished residue—the gold melted and ran between the stones! Not one stone was left upon another lest even a little precious metal be lost.

Jesus' dreadful prophecy came true—"they will not leave one stone upon another"—not because God was happy to see His people destroyed. No! He came to save them from this inevitable end.

Their house was left unto them "desolate" because they did not recognize the time of His visitation. They hid their eyes and remained unprepared. They rejected the spirit and power of Elijah; the forerunner would have made them "ready to go" for the visitation of God; the time of visitation includes the season of preparation.

Jesus says, "They have done with him whatever they decided." They had rejected His prophets in the past, and John was their last call. The people exercised their wills against God's preparation ministry instead of exercising their wills to embrace the pathway prepared before Messiah.

However, soon after the Resurrection, God molded a new remnant with the spirit and power of Elijah and the anointing of Jesus' ministry. Prophetic leadership was one of the foundations upon which He built His Church. The Church did not leave anything of God's eternal purpose behind but walked into the fullness Jesus provided. Jesus bestowed a fulfilling leadership—He fulfilled prophet, priest, and king and released it upon the Church through the fivefold leadership of His Body.

RECEIVING OR REJECTING?

The rejection of John was the rejection of Jesus. Here is the difficult aspect of prophetic leadership—because the leaders are sent to prepare for the next level and the next wave, rejecting their leadership is a rejection of the One we are being prepared to receive.

Jesus says:

"Anyone who receives you receives Me, and anyone who receives Me receives the One who sent Me.

Anyone who receives a prophet as a prophet will receive a prophet's reward, and anyone who receives a righteous person as a righteous person will receive a righteous person's reward." (See Matthew 10:40-41.)

Receive Jesus? Receive the prophet He sends. To receive Jesus, don't reject the ones He sends. One of the most rebellious things a Christian can say is, "if God has anything to say, He can say it to me. I don't need leaders to tell me what God says."

God is the One with the prophetic strategy. He sends you prophetic leaders because you need them, and He will not unlock the depths of your destiny in another way just because you don't wish to listen to His prophets.

Rejecting God-sent leaders rejects the One who sent them, and essentially rejects the hidden destiny, anointing, leadership, and ministry they release into our lives. God sends prophetic leaders to get a people ready for Him because that people will not be prepared without these leaders.

In John's day, the die was cast before Jesus was revealed. Jesus' teaching and ministry would not be received because John's was not received. This is background for everything He did and the methods by which He did them. He spoke in parables and they could not understand His Kingdom message because they were not a prophetically prepared people. The failure of Israel's leaders to receive John's ministry, to prepare themselves in the spirit and power of Elijah, set aside Jesus' ministry from the very beginning.

In many nations of the earth, increased prophetic awareness has opened the door to voices that do not reflect God's spirit and power. Strange voices are speaking in our day, as they were in John's day. Strange voices do not provide a satisfactory defense for ignoring God's voice.

The protection Jesus gave us against false prophecy was not rejection of all prophecy; Jesus gave us Holy Spirit through whom we discern God's voice and voices communicating human and demonic ideas.

The important principle—the presence of false prophets does not create an excuse for ignoring true prophets. None of us can afford to ignore God's sent ones. Ignoring the new prophetic leaders because we know some false ones leaves us further away from fulfilling God's purpose.

Ask yourself this question: "Is this all the enemy has to do to get me to reject the move of God?"

As mentioned previously, the spirit and power of Elijah prepares a people ready to receive the Lord. That's the reason for the preparation—we will recognize Jesus, the Truth, because we are prepared!

John says, "Dear friends, stop believing every spirit. Instead, test the spirits to see whether they are from God because many false prophets have gone out into the world." (See 1 John 4:1.)

A direct connection is made between prophetic preparation and recognizing the move of God. Some spirits are from God! But every spirit who does not acknowledge Jesus is not from God and this is the antichrist spirit.

John says, "You have heard that antichrist is coming, and now he is already in the world. Little children, you belong to God and have overcome, because the one who is in you is greater than the one who is in the world. These people belong to the world. That is why they speak from the world's perspective, and the world listens to them." (See 1 John 4:3-5.)

It is not something you know or have learned mentally that prepares you to recognize Him. It is Someone within you to whom you have learned to listen. Prophetic people are people who live "Spirit First."

The apostle John says, "We belong to God. The person who knows God listens to us. Whoever does not belong to God does not listen to us. This is how we know the Spirit of truth and the spirit of deceit" (1 John 4:4-6). There is spiritual truth and error, but both are spiritual and require spiritual discerning, spiritual insight provided by spiritual preparation. A prophetic people will be prepared to test prophetic voices.

Becoming a Prophetic People

A major distinction should be made between leaders with revelatory gifts and prophetic leaders who operate in the spirit and power of Elijah. One appropriately and legitimately serves the Body, but the other is sent with unusual authority and power to prepare a people for the Lord. All five leadership functions operate with a blend of spiritual gifts.

Some of the prophetic ministry models emerging during the restoration and recognition of prophets were built upon a felt need to authenticate and validate prophets. It would be natural under those circumstances to exaggerate some to prove a point and to overcompensate in an effort to answer critics. However, it is time to move the pendulum back to center.

Prophetic ministries that create a desire or need for personal words soon deteriorate into silliness. When the ability to hear words of knowledge or words of wisdom becomes a means of preparing a people for ourselves, ministry ends up answering to their curiosities and flippant desires for spiritual amusement. We may be creating the need for ourselves using revelatory gifts, building a false foundation for a faulty leadership.

I believe in personal prophecy and personal prophecy is certainly scriptural.[1] God has reclaimed the prophetic ministry for His Church in this generation and sent us prophetic leaders. Prophecy is stepping up to another level with the arrival of prophetic leaders and will pull all forms of prophetic ministry up with it. I am not standing against prophetic ministry, but I am calling for its release at a higher level under prophetic leaders.

Do our prophetic operations prepare people for the Lord or simply create a need for the prophet? Is our measure of prophetic ministry a litmus test for "spirituality," that people who "really hear God" are more valuable to the Body? Are we still playing with prophecy like a new toy, or are we ready to minister, act, and operate as prophetic people following prophetic leaders?

The gift of prophecy and the ministry of the prophet are two different functions in the Body of Christ. Words of direction that call people to decisions of spiritual and natural life should come through leaders not through prophecy gift operations designed to comfort, encourage, and strengthen.

The Trap of Religious Substitution

Something happens when revolutionary revival arrives that no man can measure, understand, or control. It is simply beyond us. It is Jesus at work, Jesus in control, and Jesus releasing His decisions.

People in Jesus' day found themselves fighting with God because of their religious substitutions. The religious mind-set is a spiritual stronghold and is the most destructive of hell's operations against the ministry of Jesus.

People will find themselves focused upon their programs while failing in their ministries. They will find themselves certain in their principles while tentative in their ministries. People will find themselves comfortable with their leaders' personalities while paralyzed in their ministries. People will find themselves empowered in their purposes while sterile in their ministries.

Jesus is not looking for a Church filled with good people doing good things for good reasons. Nor will this kind of church fulfill the Great Commission. It will substitute the accumulation of believers for the Great Commission, the completion of human vision for the purpose of God, and the development of a religious subculture for the transformation of the culture.

In fact, you will be surprised to know that hell will be happy for you to accumulate believers, build big buildings, raise and spend lots of money, and provide a spiritual comfort zone for people, as long as you do little or nothing about God's purpose in your generation. The Church in the United States spent nearly a trillion dollars over twenty years; at the same time, the Church's impact upon American culture diminished and its growth as a segment of society declined.[2]

The most frightening words of the Bible are these words of Jesus, "Not everyone saying to Me 'Lord! Lord!' will enter the kingdom of the heavens, but those doing the will of My Father in Heaven. Many will say to Me on that day, 'Lord! Lord! Did we not prophesy in Your name, and in Your name throw out demons and in Your name performed many works of power?' Then I will declare to them, 'I never knew you! Depart from Me with those who work lawlessness.'" (See Matthew 7:21-23.)

"Work lawlessness?!" How can doing things in His name for His kingdom contribute to and partner with antichrist rebellion? How can we do things in His name if He doesn't even know us? How can prophecy, good works, and human efforts at "doing church" offend the heart and mind of God?

Jesus makes it very clear that not only does this happen, but many people will do this expecting a rich heavenly reward and divine recognition. There is a difference as far as eternity is from time between people doing things for God and people successfully fulfilling His strategy, design, and present priorities for their season and culture.

During Christmas, it is a tradition to exchange gifts. Friends and family usually gather together to share presents, each person giving and receiving something themselves. In every family there is usually at least one person who gives people "what they want them to have" instead of what the person wants. I'm sure you have at least one relative whose efforts at gift giving leave you wondering if the gift was intended for someone else!

As we saw in our discussion of prophetic worship and prayer, giving God "what we desire Him to have" is an activity based upon human will and purpose. God has never given up His responsibility to create worship or relinquished His orchestration of intercession. He has not replaced His leadership with man's. Jesus has not given up His responsibility to govern and guide His Kingdom. Whatever we do for Him must be a direct order from Him.

It appears Jesus is saying that it is possible to do things for God He never asked, designed, or gifted us to do, and these efforts may produce appreciable success when gauged by our instruments of measurement. This is just not the way the Kingdom operates. The Kingdom is run by the King!

God Speaks Today!

When God wants something to happen, He says something. When God wants something to happen in Heaven, He speaks. When God wants something done in the earth, He speaks. No matter what wonderful things we do for God, the fulfillment of His will and purpose is all that interests Him. Only the activities that get God what He wants receive investments of grace, anointing, and favor. This is not because of God's great selfishness; it is because of God's great, passionate love! He wants what He wants to happen!

It is possible to spend years of your life doing spiritual things for God that are worthless and meaningless while avoiding the vital and eternal destinies and purposes for which you were created. Jesus makes it clear that many people will enter eternity's last day with expectations foreign to the mind and heart of God. They are people who expended great effort and invested money, time, and strength in things "God didn't have anything to do with."

We cannot act out a man-made script with the expectation that God will be entertained and pleased. God isn't interested in watching our religious productions no matter how lavish the sets or dramatic the presentations. He will say, "Who are you and what are you doing? I didn't order this movie. Shut it off!"

Endnotes

1. God talks to individuals as well as nations, leaders, and situations. He speaks through individuals to individuals. The gift of prophecy is an individual gift we all should desire, a gift in which we all may operate. First Corinthians 14:3: "For you all may be able, released, and empowered to prophesy individually, in turn, so everyone can be heard and addressed." Personal prophecy would be hearing from God and speaking to individuals. This is evidenced by the phrase Paul uses in First Corinthians 12:25, "what is hidden in his heart." Paul says that anyone could speak prophetically and reveal unseen, unknown heart issues. I am not saying, however, that any Christian can prophesy anytime to any person; this ignores protocols of personal prophecy.

2. The State of the Church, 2002, George Barna. "It is quite astounding that although Protestant and Catholic churches have raised—and spent—close to one trillion dollars on domestic ministry during the past two decades, there has been no measurable increase in one of the expressed purposes of the church: to lead people to Christ and have them commit their lives to Him." Barna Update, June 4, 2002: "Layer on top of that the fact that churches have raised and spent more than $500 billion dollars in the past decade to try to influence America's spiritual life and it seems pretty obvious that it takes more than good intentions and a menu of popular programs to make a dent in the nation's religious identity and consciousness."

Conclusion

Revival and Restoration

Hear the Word of the Lord! Nations of the earth, Someone is coming! Heaven is visiting earth in unlikely places at unlikely times. God wishes His visit to be received properly, and even now He sends special representatives ahead of Him to prepare His people.

He must have a Church with a prophetic nature. God is raising the level of prophetic experience for His people. The level of spiritual experience that's coming is unusual, so God is giving us a foretaste of that next season prophetically. He wants us ready when He comes to visit!

One touchstone of Pentecost was revelation that flowed into and through the Church: "Upon all flesh I will gush out My Spirit. No matter what age, social status, gender, or maturity of that flesh, people will see visions and dream dreams and prophesy." (See Acts 2:17.)

That is why, right now, God is shaking the nations, calling His people to radical transformation. History's greatest harvest must be properly gathered. The spirit and power of Elijah is absolutely necessary to prepare all the Church for all God is doing.

John the Baptist certainly fulfilled his charge as a transformational leader; his nation was stirred, its foundations and institutions shaken, and great crowds of people were sincerely seeking by the time Jesus was introduced as the Lamb of God. John revealed the heart of the Father, the deep longing Father has to visit His people. John revealed that God wanted to visit Israel without crushing them. John's ministry was one of preparation, a revelation of the coming move of God, and the present need for radical personal change.

Later moves of God came to New Testament cities like Ephesus, Antioch, and Samaria. God has visited regions of the earth in modern times including six great awakening moves of God in the United States. These moves of God have swept thousands into the Kingdom. God has visited cities and regions of South America and Africa, cities like Toronto in Canada and Pensacola in the United States. I believe that God is still visiting places in the earth, and will do so with greater frequency and increased intensity in this generation.

God sent John to Israel with a message of restoration and mercy; He did not want to destroy Israel in the opportunity of her greatest fulfillment. He wanted to fully restore the very purpose for which He had chosen and redeemed her.

John calls a culture designed and destined to release Messiah's Kingdom to the whole earth, he calls them back to their cultural purpose, to the fulfillment of their national destiny. John calls a people far from that fulfillment, on the brink of failure; and his call awakens the hearts of a remnant. John's message is heard by those who have ears to hear.

Revival and Restoration

In any place where the spirit and power of Elijah is released, God will call all of His people; however, a remnant will hear His voice and respond first. When revival comes, unprepared people misunderstand it.

Jesus came to His own, and His own received Him not. When Jesus comes to nations, many people within the conventional church will miss Him because He will look, sound, and act differently than they have imagined, differently than the atmosphere of comfort and the form of religion that dominates so much of Christianity. The religious spirit resists and rejects the power of the Spirit.

The entire Church is called to prepare, but a prophetic remnant will emerge, a people who hear the call of restoration. The remnant is not supposed to "go it alone" just because they hear it first. They continue reaching out, calling, and praying for the remainder of the Church. The remnant is not the elite core. They are first fruits of a greater response.

God is restoring all to the Church in the spirit and power of Elijah. All that the Church received from Jesus, from Pentecost, from the apostles and prophets of her foundations, is being restored. The spirit and power of Elijah operates as restoration leadership, as prophetic leadership normal to the New Testament.

Revival Fire

Great Awakening Revival occurs when the move of God among a prepared people extends into the general population; great awakening creates a heightened awareness of God and spiritual issues among the whole culture, an unexplained turning of minds and hearts toward God among the people outside the Church.

This awakening can only be understood from a spiritual point of view. It is completely out of the control of men. The move of God draws people toward salvation. The Gospel's power to transform vastly increases, the effectiveness of ministry accelerates, and thousands turn to Jesus Christ because it is Kingdom Gospel.

In previous times of awakening, strong manifestations of spiritual power were evidenced; people fell to the ground under strong conviction of sin and the awe of God. When they found peace and joy, they expressed themselves in ways new and novel to the established church, offending some Christians with the fervor and passion of their new life in Christ.

People who initially reject any new expression may not be bad people. They may simply be unprepared for what God is doing. Without proper prophetic preparation, the Church may find itself fighting against the very thing God is doing in their generation because it looks and sounds different from their present pre-set, comfort-zone spirituality.

My wife and I were engaged in ministry for more than 25 years with little prophetic preparation. I preached *against* what I am now! During a very dark and difficult time in our ministry, having lost everything, God miraculously brought us into one of this generation's most powerful revivals and totally transformed our lives!

While it was hard to admit that we had been wrong all those years, and difficult to consider starting over again in ministry, God mercifully prepared us for His visitation so we can be part of the greatest harvest in history. Now it's your turn!

Get Ready!

God has begun the period of preparation. He has moved the spiritual thermostat across the nation up several degrees already, and things are heating up. During these first few years of the new millennium, new leaders are emerging and existing leaders are being transformed.

People are now experiencing revolutionary revival who say, "If you had told me two years ago I would be like this, I would have said you were crazy!"

Especially telling of this move of God are existing leaders who are displaced or forced to start over in new contexts of ministry. Many prophetic leaders will discover something within them they didn't know was there, a leadership anointing that doesn't match their present positions. They will be transformed for revolutionary revival. What they considered their lifelong ministry niche will suddenly be too small, too boring, and too comfortable! Existing leaders will be transformed to lead the church to the next level.

Revolutionary revival first touches an awakened remnant responding to transformed leaders who "go before Him in the spirit and power of Elijah." Revolutionary revival then creates radical change, stirs opposition, and appears to separate the remnant from "normal Christianity."

A price is paid by every existing leader who embraces the move of God. Because it is unusual and radical, prophetic leadership challenges establishments of religion and the status quo of the church. "John the Baptist leaders" standing up now to declare revolutionary revival will certainly attract the attention of scoffers; but it is, at the same moment, very difficult to deny the reality of fire. Whether fire is accepted or rejected, it demands some response from all who experience it because it is God's fire!

Jesus has given more than a century to restoring the fullness of the Church. It is now fully available in and through the Church but cannot be successfully implemented without transformation because the ministry of Jesus cannot properly be executed without the disposition of Jesus. You can't do what Jesus did until you become who Jesus is.

Prophetic leadership is transformational leadership, and transformational leadership is necessary to the fullest restoration of the ministry of Jesus. Prophetic leaders cannot lead without prophetic people; and prophetic people cannot be prepared unless they are personally, internally, and spiritually transformed.

This is the spirit and power of Elijah: the release of God's fire consuming the rebuilt altars of covenant, commitment, and consecration until nothing remains but Him. John's message was clear: "Someone else is coming who will immerse you in Holy Spirit fire. He stands with a fan at the threshing floor of your lives to blow the husks into a consuming fire. He will not stop until the grain is completely free of worthless husks." (See Matthew 3:11-12.)

In biblical times, harvested grain would be piled on a stone floor. One person would create a strong breeze on one side with a large fan while someone else would throw the grain up in the air. The breeze from this fan would gust through the grain and the worthless husks would be blown into a fire on the opposite side.

John's picture of Jesus' ministry shows what He will do when He claims His Church. Something is destroyed in redemption. Something is redeemed. Jesus won't stop until He has redeemed the precious and destroyed the worthless in His people.

Revival Prioritizes the Church

Traveling around Brazil, Ruthanne and I have seen the strength of this fire, the passion released in the young and old. It is the fire of revival. It is real! This is not a move of God for a few odd people located on the fringe of the Church. God has sent Brazil forerunning leaders to prepare people all over that nation for this great move of God. A remnant matrix is growing as Christians are praying and worshiping at a new level.

Brazil, like many other nations, has waited centuries for this moment, and this generation is going to see with their own eyes and hear with their own ears the fulfillment of cultural purpose!

Brazil is certainly one revival nation, the focus of Heaven's investment of power and authority! But Brazil is not the only one. Get ready China, India, the Philippines! Get ready nations of destiny! Someone is coming!

Many of us would say, "I would like to invest the best of my years and ministry in the nations where God is moving in revival." Of course we would. While a faithful continuity is necessary in every place at every moment wherever God positions His servants, the Church should be able to discern the coming moves of God and turn her resources toward the cultures and cities where God is moving in revival. Since these are God's priorities, they should become the priorities of the whole Body.

The resources of the whole Body should be turned toward God's priorities. God makes His priorities known by His visits. Where is God opening a door? Where is God renewing a culture's purposes, awakening a sleeping Church, pouring a purifying presence? The whole Church will be filled with the knowledge of the glory of the Lord, and the whole earth will be covered with this knowledge as well—when the prepared Church responds to Jesus' priorities.

The Church should know "the ball of the time" and target existing leaders Jesus is lifting up to take the church to the next level. We must discover the emerging leaders He is raising up in preparation for the next wave and help release them with momentum.

The angel Gabriel announced such a visitation was coming to Israel, that the baby born to Zachariah and Elizabeth would "go ahead of Him" to prepare people "in the spirit and power of Elijah." This same anointing is available in the nations where God is coming—a prophetic anointing upon prophetic leaders for restoration and transformation.

APPENDIX

The Vision of Jesus Claiming His Church

Jesus Standing Up

March 7, 2003. While teaching a class on spiritual warfare, preparing the class for intercession, we were worshiping together listening to a song, "Ask for the Nations," and prophetic anointing came over me—powerfully—for more than one hour. In this defining moment, I understood some of what God is up to in the nations, and how I would need to relate my ministry and life to fulfill my own destiny in concert with fulfilling His purposes.

I want to relate the vision here because it set many things in motion that speak to the thesis of this book; more, that speaks to the heart of God for here and now.

It was Friday morning. We were worshipping together before the teaching when the Spirit began to speak prophetically and I saw an open vision. The following is a portion of that prophetic experience.

The Calling

"'Deep calls to deep.' 'Deep calls to deep.' Go into the depths of your spirit man—the depths of God and the depths of your spirit—the depths of the hidden places normally not visible, hidden places within you where God operates. It is out of these spiritual places hidden things emerge and are revealed. Something deeper and hidden operates beyond what your eyes are accustomed to seeing. In those places, God works most.

"'Deep calls to deep.' God sometimes pulls back the curtain and allows you to see this matrix, a crucible of spiritual release. Now is such a time. Holy Spirit is searching the deep. Searching. Working within you.

"God is reaching into deep wells He has stored up, sources put within you in preparation for this day. What He has stored, He is now going to use—coming up from your spirit. Holy Spirit is bringing resources, for God has put something within you that you did not know was there. He put it there. He brings it up. God has had these things stored for such a time as this, and for such a people as this."

God Standing Up as a Warrior

"I see the Lord rousing Himself as a Mighty Warrior, rousing Himself in power and authority. He is awesome, as the Scriptures say, terrible in the sense that He creates terror and awe in those who witness His presence and character.

"He is shaking Himself, shaking off what He allowed to settle around and upon Him, conditions allowed to continue in His mercy, to settle upon the earth, to remain in place to be awakened in a new season. Jesus is beginning to shake Himself and shake off these conditions. These conditions are temporal, natural, and earthly. They rested

The Vision of Jesus Claiming His Church

upon Him as sifting dust settles upon an immobile object."

[I was hovering over South America. I could sense that Jesus was lying down there, covered with the dust of centuries. Waiting. As I watched, He stood up and shook Himself. The wind blew away the dust as if it had never been.]

"He is shaking Himself, roused as the Psalmist says, 'Stand up, Oh God!' He is standing. The dust of centuries is shaking loose from His body and a mighty wind blows it away as if it had never been.

"It is not that He has been inactive. Scriptures describe these kairos times as 'days of the Lord.' We are approaching another 'day of the Lord' in history when God is revealed and His purposes are reestablished. He is revealing Himself among the nations, and the hearts of many will be shaken. Men will be weak with terror at what God is about to do.

[Jesus was standing up now. He set His feet and looked around challenging everything and everyone. His eyes were flames of fire and He was dressed as a warrior. He was claiming the land for His Kingdom purposes! As He challenged all other claims, mighty angels began standing up all over South America, Central America, and into the United States.]

"As the Lord is rising, mighty angels are rising all around Him, rising with Him. He is Lord of hosts, Lord of armies. Rising with Him are dormant conditions, not really dormant as much as they have been simply hidden. They have remained 'in the depths' but are now coming to the surface. This is happening in every nation of the earth, but especially in the Americas—Central and South America extending into North America."

ANGELIC MOVEMENTS IN THE WESTERN HEMISPHERE

"Among nations of South America, moving north through Central America, through Mexico into New Mexico, and then northeast into the very heartland of the United States, the arising angelic army is moving. I can see a map of this terrain with angels standing up in strategic locations, first in Brazil, then standing up progressively in Central America, Mexico, New Mexico, and arising in the heartland states of the United States. Angels of cities and nations are standing tall in power and authority, rising up one after the other!

"Angels of the Lord are rousing. They are responding to the Mighty Warrior who is shaking Himself. He stands up in this day for His purposes, they stand with Him. He is a mighty and awesome God!

"If you will reach into the depths, you will begin to feel a response within you. This is the sense of 'deep calling unto deep' I am hearing today. In the remnant, there is a response, in the faithful there is a response, something automatic. His call begins to resonate within your spirit. You respond because your spirit man has the same seeds of God's life that are within the angels answering His initiatives. The very same spiritual force causing angels in these regions to stand causes a response in the faithful remnant across the same geographic terrain."

THE BRIDGE BETWEEN THE AMERICAS

"As He rouses Himself, you are roused! You begin to stir. Something you might not have known was within

The Vision of Jesus Claiming His Church

responds to this day of the Lord! There is more within you than you know! There is a great strength and power God has reserved.

"When God moves, His people respond. They respond to Him. A cord stretches from the heart of God to the heart of His remnant. As God pulls, that string strains with purpose and they respond with Him.

"Jesus is stirring Himself. Jesus is stirring in the Americas. God is stirring that spirit released for destiny and purpose—of redemptive purpose. Especially I see this purpose running through the heart of South America in Brazil. It is this sense of God's heart in the hearts of nations that plays on the word *heartland* in both continents and walks the bridge between them. Central America is the bridge between the heart of God for each northern and southern continent.

"I hear this word *Tegucigalpa*. I see ley lines[1] drawn where the angels rise up, lines of spiritual strength and power moving to forge a 'line of strength' all the way from Brazil through the bridge of Central America and into New Mexico.

"God is talking about this connection, and now I see it connects the Northeastern part of New Mexico and extends into the heart of America."

Power and Prophetic Revelation

"This connection has to do with what God released at the beginning of the last century, what we called the Pentecostal Movement. This is a continuing of that move of God, renewing and releasing something into the earth.

"It is stirring within the Church, the deep of God calls to the deep of your own spirit. It does not matter how long you have been filled with the Spirit, something in the depths of God continues to cry for greater release.

"The depths of God are speaking to the depths of man. What is there is being stirred again. God will establish another Azusa Street. He will create another place in another time when He forcefully releases His Spirit with power and revelation. He is continuing that initial release, not just of its power, but of its revelation.

"God is sending the power of His Spirit accompanied by the prophetic; revelation is arising with the power. God began in Topeka not only with power and gifts but with the prophetic. This combined release has withered because of human concerns, but God is saying, 'I rouse myself to stand up in the power of the Spirit with the prophetic, Word and Spirit at the same time. This release will cause my logos mind-set to be exalted. A place of revelation comes upon my people to read in the same Word a greater revelation of the depths of the Spirit.

"It is 'depth.' A greater depth of revelation and understanding is becoming available from the same Word. He promises in the last days that those who arise in response to God rousing Himself will have understanding of events in the daily news, and that God is raising up a generation.

"He wants you to have wisdom to understand what it is He is up to in the earth as you respond to His shaking. He is saying to this remnant as He said to Abraham, 'will I do something in the earth and not talk to my friend, Abraham?'

The Vision of Jesus Claiming His Church

"He is saying, 'I am about to do a thing in the earth that will make the ears of men tingle and make the hearts of men fail. But I am not going to do that before I have talked to my people. My friends of the earth and I are about to have conversations, about to reach an understanding. I am taking them to a place of revelation they have not been before.' Those who have the response of God in the deep of their spirits will rise up; and as God is shaking and shaking dust off Himself to stand, they will shake themselves and shake dust off themselves to stand. They will shake off the dust of the past that has settled upon them."

God's Authority Established

"Now I see God's warrior armor. I see underneath this armor His spiritual might. God has arisen, standing tall for His purposes, and I see more clearly now His posture."

[I could see Jesus more clearly and distinctly now. I was focused in on Him. God began to highlight parts of His Body to me like a graphic and enlarge them before my spiritual eyes—His armor, shoulders and neck, His heart beating within His chest—giving me insights to the meaning of the vision. It was so intense! Everything about Jesus, Lord of Heaven and Earth, is too big for my mind! I understand why prophetic people in scriptural accounts would fall down as dead men. God is overwhelming!]

"I am seeing God's shoulders. I am seeing His shoulders as the place of government or authority. I see God shaking Himself. He is strong and mighty in His shoulders. He is strong and mighty in His chest and arms as well, but He has extremely broad shoulders with powerful muscles at the neck, the muscles that turn the Head, powerful muscles at the neck that hold the neck erect and strong. These muscles stabilize the head and keep the eyes focused, so that as the neck is stable the eyes are stabilized to see not only near but far away.

"To see long distances, we must have stability. Even the tiniest movements and instabilities distort long-range vision. Telescopes and high-powered binoculars must often be stabilized on tripods and stands. The more distant the vision, the more stability is required by the visual aid. God's neck stabilizes His head and long-range vision is clear. God is standing up to extend clear, long-range vision to this generation.

"God is standing with strong shoulders to establish His government, but the strong shoulders include strong muscles to stabilize the head for long-range prophetic vision and accuracy.

"I see that the heart of God is strong, beating strong. He stands up to accept and assume authority because His shoulders are strong to bear that government. He is the God of government. He is the God of order. He is the God of wisdom and revelation.

"Apostles and prophets are the foundations of the Church. The apostolic and prophetic are arising in the Americas, bringing a stabilizing order to the Body so that the prophetic vision may be long-range and accurate, creating an understanding that moves the responding people of God toward the purposes for which He stands up and establishes His government."

The Vision of Jesus Claiming His Church

The Response of God's People

"He says, 'This word is My word, and I am about to shake Myself as I stand in this place of revelation as I rouse Myself and shake what has settled during the prolonged time of mercy. As I rouse myself, you must also rouse yourself.'

"You will be roused as you answer and respond to the call of God. That rousing will occur in the very depths of who you are. 'As you are roused in response to me,' God says, 'I will raise up angelic armies.'

"God is raising up mighty angels, responding in concert with God's people. Heavenly armies support earthly armies.

[In the vision, God spoke directly to me as His friend. His voice changed to explain and mentor. I know very little about angels and still know very little about them. He was not making me an angel expert as much as He was explaining something I needed to understand to make sense of the vision.]

"'You often understand that I would send angels, and you see Me sending angels from Heaven, but I want you to understand today that there are angels in residence, angels who have been assigned, angels who have been at their posts awaiting this day of the Lord, that I am rousing up from where they are.'

"In this army God establishes order and government of these angelic hosts who have been in position for centuries. These ancient warriors who have been in place are rousing themselves, stirring themselves.

"'I am not so much sending from Heaven as I am rousing what has been in residence, waiting and ready for this generation. I am rousing mighty warring angels, and these angels are standing in their places in the Americas. I have been putting these angelic hosts in place for this time.'

"You have read in My Word how one of My angels puts one foot in the land and one foot on the sea and says, 'Time is no more!' The time is used up and reached its end! Now is such a moment, a kairos time. I planned for this season, and now is the time.

"He says, 'This angel's declaration is a picture of what I am doing now. I am stirring angels who will stand up and place one foot on the land and one foot on the sea in places of the earth and in individual nations.' The angel will say, 'The time is used up; the time has run its course; time has brought us to giving birth.'

[Now I see a close up of Jesus' face filled with passion and fire. He is opening His mouth to roar—the Lion is roaring!—and I know the shout of the Lord will release something of what I have seen in His heart. I know it is the passion of Jesus for the purposes of God. I see His shout as fire coming from His mouth, the outflow and overflow of the burning passion of His heart for Father's will to be done. He is releasing this passion into the Americas. It is a generation of passionate people!]

"I see the Lord who is standing now beginning to open His mouth. As He opens His mouth, He releases a great shout. First, a great shout, a thundering comes out of His mouth from the depths of God, releasing through the mouth of God what is hidden in His heart. But after the great shout, after the voice, His mouth opens again and is filled with fire. His mouth releases fire upon the earth. That fire is trouble for those who are wood, hay and stubble; and that fire is refining and enriching for those who respond from the depths of their spirits to the depths of God's heart. The remnant shall find in that fire a place of great power, purity, and focus. The purity and focus will be single-mindedness, a focus of oneness and singleness in their hearts toward God.

"The Lord says, 'As I shout and release fire from my mouth. I will thunder. Am I not 'The Lord,' and is not my name 'The Lord' for a reason? When I respond to the events of time, when history advances, do I not respond from who I am that arises from the depths of God?

"I am responding to the Father's purposes, and from the perspective of His purposes I change Heaven and earth, move Heaven and earth, shake Heaven and earth. I will speak from Heaven into earth and that which has been bound and loosed in Heaven, in earth shall be bound and loosed. My voice will shake loose and My voice will bind up. I will release into the nations of the earth in this kairos time a renewing of their redemptive purposes!

[Jesus is revealing reality to me. What is real to Him becomes real to me, a picture of spiritual reality. He points out the strategic particulars progressively released in this time. I see the mighty angels and their terrible authority and power in the spirit. I see their equipment and armament.]

"'This is the day of the opportunity. When the shaking comes, I will redistribute. Some will be raised and some lowered; some will be lifted and some destroyed. But in this time of shaking and redistributing I will establish something that you have never seen in the earth: a changing of the guard. Angels of the Lord stand and in their hands—see, their hands are not empty!—but in their hands are great swords, great swords!'

"The sword of the Lord is for dividing, for distinguishing, for differentiating. It draws a line in the sand. It divides asunder. His Word separates soul and spirit, which divides between joints and marrow.

"Jesus says, 'I will divide. I will separate. I will distinguish and differentiate. I will cause there to be a revelation of which is and that which is not, of that which has been hidden and that which has been revealed. I will cause men and women to understand where they stand with respect to my purposes, hidden but now revealed.'

"There will be a division in the earth. I said while I was here: 'I came to bring a sword and I came to bring a division.' It is not because I do not like peace, but because there must be a distinguishing, a differentiation in the time of battle. You must know the enemy. There must be recognition of the enemy, and recognition of God's friends. You must know the battle. When the battle is set in array, you must understand who is on the Lord's side, who is on the Lord's side!

"The Lord says, 'I rouse myself as a Mighty Warrior now. And as I shout, the first response of the people in the earth must be, 'who is on the Lord's side? Who is on the Lord's side?' The Lord knows and others will know who is on His side. It will be obvious in both Heaven and earth who is on the Lord's side.

The Vision of Jesus Claiming His Church

"God says, 'As the angels of hell have raised themselves up against Me, now I rouse Myself, a Mighty Warrior against them. I come not empty-handed, and I come not without angels, not without an army of angels! I come equipped. I come ready. I do not come alone. I have mighty angels in place who have been hidden from the hoards of hell who do not understand what I have had in place. Now they are caught unaware. They laugh in this day of battle, for they believe they have already put themselves in a position of victory, but I have hidden weapons. I have depths of God they do not know. Hell even thinks that the church, especially in North America, is so asleep that it cannot be raised. Because it is so dead, it cannot be resurrected.'

"The Lord says, 'I have in the depths of My people something hell does not understand. I have in the depths of My people something My people do not understand. I am God! I have not come to this moment unprepared! I will reach into the depths of Myself; I will reach into the depths of My people. The response will shake Heaven and earth! It will cause men and women to stand in places of strength and leadership. Government that is upon My shoulders will then rest on the shoulders of men and women I have prepared.

"'So, do not say in this day of battle, I am too weak. Do not say in this day of victory, I lack wisdom to govern!

"'I know who My Gideon's are; I know who My Solomon's are; I know who My David's are; I know who My Moses' are; I know who My Abraham's are! Do not say of yourself, because you look at the flesh, 'I am not ready.'

"'Am I unable? For I am the Lord of Heaven and earth, and I am the Lord of you! To those I place in powerful positions I release a grace-flow of wisdom, an understanding heart for what I have released into the depths of their lives. The call that I have given them will be so real and powerful within them they will recognize that what I have set in place, what I have begun, I will finish!'"

Endnote

1. Ley lines are patterns of geographic interest or significance based upon markers such as mountains, rivers, monuments, boundaries, roads, or cities. Ley lines have prophetic significance and God speaks to us through these symbolic patterns. Many are archeologically significant because the spiritual conditions they represent as historic to the land. Spiritual conditions are tied to cultural and geographic conditions. Do not confuse this discussion with new age practices anymore than you confuse psychics with prophets. However, do not dismiss this discussion because the strategy of hell is to claim land through demonic sites, idolatry, Masonic marking and mapping, for example. Ley lines are valid discussions for spiritual warfare. Some discussions go back to the early church and the practice of destroying idolatrous and pagan markings, replacing and redeeming them with Christian symbols.

Ministry Information

Don and Ruthanne Lynch have more than 35 years of ministry experience. Since they experienced revolutionary revival in Pensacola, Florida, their lives and ministry have been radically transformed. They immediately began a journey of accelerated training in the Spirit, developing skills in intercession, prophetic ministry, and apostolic leadership. Don completed an additional doctorate with Wagner Leadership Institute, exposing his ministry to international leaders in deliverance and spiritual warfare, intercession, prophecy, leadership development, and apostolic ministry. He continues to be a student of revolutionary revival and reformation.

Don has developed ministries that identify, prepare, and release leaders. These ministries have a proven track record of ministry training. His international discipling and leadership development ministry, called Freedom-Ministry has impacted tens of thousands in the United States and Brazil.

Ministry Matrix, the Lynch's international home base, nourishes and connects a growing network of ministry leaders. FreedomMinistry provides a two-year discipling pathway to spiritual maturity for local expressions of the Body of Christ. David's Army is a Northeast Florida initiative for revolutionary revival leaders who, like David's mighty men, anticipate what is coming next for the Church.

Don and Ruthanne have trained hundreds of leaders in intercession and transformational discipling and travel with trained teams in the nations. They are currently building apostolic resource centers in Jacksonville, Florida, and Sao Paulo, Brazil, to serve leaders Jesus is raising for revolutionary revival in these strategic, trend-setting cities.

For more information about Dr. Don and Ruthanne Lynch, their ministries, scheduling, or materials, please e-mail: ministrymatrix@comcast.net.

Or write to:

Dr. Don Lynch/Ministry Matrix
12146 Millford Lane North
Jacksonville, FL 32246
Telephone: 904-463-0196
Website: www.ministrymatrix.com

Ministry Resources

Teaching CDs

The Spirit & Power of Elijah

This is live teaching on the revelation discussed in this book presented at a conference in Florida. Don teaches about prophetic leadership and the strategy of Jesus for His Church in this season. These messages have been preached to more than 100,000 leaders. They are messages to the Church Body, and a message to the nations.

David's Mighty Men

Six CDs about revolutionary revival leaders. The new prophetic leaders are being prepared in the wilderness, hidden from conventional church. They are men and women misunderstood and sometimes rejected by "what is" because they are already living "what is coming next" for the Church.

Failure

What you are calling "failure" is God's greatest opportunity for your personal growth, your next step in destiny, and your open door to destiny fulfillment. Stop staring at it, and start overcoming today!

Suffering

Do you know that the Bible word for *suffering* also means "passion"? Start pushing past the limitations by releasing your passion. People spend millions on motivational tools, but Christians have the greatest motivational power in the universe available in their spirits—the passion of God!

The Cycle of Bitterness

Bitterness is a spiritual condition especially prevalent in the modern church in the United States. Bitterness comes from a false sense of loss, that something was lost that "was never mine" in the first place. A false sense of loss comes from false expectations. The cycle of bitterness must be broken by forgiveness and surrender. Tens of thousands of Christians walk this dead-end track over and over, moving from leader to leader, church to church, relationship to relationship, looking for something they will never find and blaming others, themselves, and God for the loss. Two CDs.

Hypocrisy

Appearances are the staple of modern Christianity. Jesus went to the root of religious performance when He uncovered the hypocrites in His generation. You need to deal with every religious behavior in your life, move past appearances, and live in the reality of His authority and power.

Additional copies of this book and other book titles from DESTINY IMAGE are available at your local bookstore.

Call toll-free: 1-800-722-6774.

Send a request for a catalog to:

Destiny Image® Publishers, Inc.
P.O. Box 310
Shippensburg, PA 17257-0310

"Speaking to the Purposes of God for this Generation and for the Generations to Come."

**For a complete list of our titles,
visit us at www.destinyimage.com.**